Dreamweaver Basic

Student Manual

Australia • Canada • Mexico • Singapore
Spain • United Kingdom • United States

Dreamweaver 3.0: Basic

VP and GM of Courseware:	Michael Springer
Series Product Managers:	Caryl Bahner-Guhin, Charles G. Blum, and Adam A. Wilcox
Developmental Editor:	Jim O'Shea
Production Editor:	Ellina Beletsky
Project Editor:	Richard P. Flanagan
Series Designer:	Adam A. Wilcox
Cover Designer:	Efrat Reis

COPYRIGHT © 2001 Course Technology, a division of Thomson Learning. Thomson Learning is a trademark used herein under license.

ALL RIGHTS RESERVED. No part of this work may be reproduced, transcribed, or used in any form or by any means—graphic, electronic, or mechanical, including photocopying, recording, taping, Web distribution, or information storage and retrieval systems—without the prior written permission of the publisher.

For more information contact:

Course Technology ILT
22 Thomson Place
Boston, MA 02210

Or find us on the Web at: www.course.com

For permission to use material from this text or product, contact us by
• Web: www.thomsonrights.com
• Phone: 1-800-730-2214
• Fax: 1-800-730-2215

Trademarks

Course ILT is a trademark of Course Technology.

Some of the product names and company names used in this book have been used for identification purposes only and may be trademarks or registered trademarks of their respective manufacturers and sellers.

Disclaimer

Course Technology reserves the right to revise this publication and make changes from time to time in its content without notice.

ISBN 0-619-01420-2

Printed in the United States of America

2 3 4 5 MZ 04 03 02 01 00

Contents

Introduction   iii
Topic A: About the manual... iv
Topic B: Setting your expectations.. vii
Topic C: Re-keying the course xi

Getting started with Dreamweaver 3.0   1-1
Topic A: Defining the Internet and HTML Basics........................... 1-2
Topic B: Exploring the Dreamweaver 3.0 environment 1-4
Topic C: Working with documents.. 1-14
Unit summary: Getting started with Dreamweaver 3.0.................. 1-21

Creating Web pages   2-1
Topic A: Creating documents 2-2
Topic B: Enhancing documents 2-5
Unit summary: Creating Web pages 2-11

Enhancing documents   3-1
Topic A: Formatting documents 3-2
Topic B: Checking the spelling... 3-12
Topic C: Importing text 3-14
Unit summary: Enhancing documents 3-18

Designing a site   4-1
Topic A: Creating sites 4-2
Topic B: Working with the Site window 4-5
Topic C: Working with site maps 4-10
Topic D: Working with templates... 4-12
Unit summary: Designing a site.. 4-19

Connecting Web pages   5-1
Topic A: Linking pages.. 5-2
Topic B: Creating links using named anchors 5-9
Topic C: Linking to Web sites and e-mail addresses...................... 5-15
Unit summary: Connecting Web pages.. 5-17

Working with images   6-1
Topic A: Inserting an image in a document 6-2
Topic B: Adding background images 6-8
Topic C: Creating links by using images.. 6-10
Unit summary: Working with images.. 6-16

Creating tables 7-1

Topic A: Adding tables 7-2
Topic B: Formatting tables... 7-11
Topic C: Resizing cells and tables... 7-17
Topic D: Using tables to design Web pages... 7-22
Unit summary: Creating tables... 7-28

Creating frames and uploading sites 8-1

Topic A: Working with frames.. 8-2
Topic B: Modifying frames... 8-12
Topic C: Uploading sites... 8-18
Unit summary: Creating frames and uploading sites....................................... 8-27

Course summary S-1

Topic A: Course summary... S-2
Topic B: Continued learning after class S-4

Quick reference Q-1

Index I-1

Dreamweaver 3.0: Basic

Introduction

After reading this introduction, you will know how to:

A Use Course Technology ILT manuals in general.

B Use prerequisites, a target student description, course objectives, and a skills inventory to set your expectations for the course.

C Re-key this course after class.

Topic A: About the manual

Course Technology ILT philosophy

Course Technology ILT manuals facilitate your learning by providing structured interaction with the software itself. While we provide text to explain difficult concepts, the hands-on activities are the focus of our courses. By paying close attention as your instructor leads you through these activities, you will learn the skills and concepts effectively.

We believe strongly in the instructor-led classroom. During class, focus on your instructor. Our manuals are designed and written to facilitate your interaction with your instructor, and not to call attention to the manuals themselves.

We believe in the basic approach of setting expectations, delivering instruction, and providing summary and review afterwards. For this reason, lessons begin with objectives and end with summaries. We also provide overall course objectives and a course summary to provide both an introduction to and closure of the entire course.

Manual components

The manuals contain these major components:

1 Table of contents
2 Introduction
3 Units
4 Course summary
5 Reference
6 Index

Each element is described below.

Table of contents

The table of contents acts as a learning roadmap.

Introduction

The introduction contains information about our training philosophy and our manual components, features, and conventions. It contains target student, prerequisite, objective, and setup information for the specific course.

Units

Units are the largest structural component of the course content. A unit begins with a title page that lists objectives for each major subdivision, or topic, within the unit. Within each topic, conceptual and explanatory information alternates with hands-on activities. Units conclude with a summary comprising one paragraph for each topic, and an independent practice activity that gives you an opportunity to practice the skills you've learned.

The conceptual information takes the form of text paragraphs, exhibits, lists, and tables. The activities are structured in two columns, one telling you what to do, the other providing explanations, descriptions, and graphics.

Course summary

This section provides a text summary of the entire course. It is useful for providing closure at the end of the course. The course summary also indicates the next course in this series, if there is one, and lists additional resources you might find useful as you continue to learn about the software.

Reference

The reference is an at-a-glance job aid summarizing some of the more common features of the software.

Index

The index enables you to quickly find information about a particular feature or concept of the software.

Manual conventions

We've tried to keep the number of elements and the types of formatting to a minimum in the manuals. This aids in clarity and makes the manuals more classically elegant looking. But there are some conventions and icons you should know about.

Convention/ Icon	Description
Italic text	In conceptual text, indicates a new term or feature.
Bold text	In unit summaries, indicates a key term or concept. In an independent practice activity, indicates an explicit item that you select, choose, or type.
`Code font`	Indicates code or syntax.
Select **bold item**	In the left column of hands-on activities, bold sans-serif text indicates an explicit item that you select, choose, or type.
Keycaps like (↵ ENTER)	Indicate a key on the keyboard you must press.

Hands-on activities

The hands-on activities are the most important parts of our manuals. They are divided into two primary columns. The "Here's how" column gives short instructions to you about what to do. The "Here's why" column provides explanations, graphics, and clarifications. Here's a sample:

Do it!

A-1:   Creating a commission formula

Here's how	Here's why
1 Open Sales	This is an oversimplified sales compensation worksheet. It shows sales totals, commissions, and incentives for five sales reps.
2 Observe the contents of cell F4	`F4` ▼ **=** `=E4*C Rate`
	The commission rate formulas use the name "C_Rate" instead of a value for the commission rate.

For these activities, we have provided a collection of data files designed to help you learn each skill in a real-world business context. As you work through the activities, you will modify and update these files. Of course, you might make a mistake and, therefore, want to re-key the activity starting from scratch. To make it easy to start over, you will rename each data file at the end of the first activity in which the file is modified. Our convention for renaming files is to add the word "My" to the beginning of the file name. In the above activity, for example, a file called "Sales" is being used for the first time. At the end of this activity, you would save the file as "My sales," thus leaving the "Sales" file unchanged. If you make a mistake, you can start over using the original "Sales" file.

In some activities, however, it may not be practical to rename the data file. If you want to retry one of these activities, ask your instructor for a fresh copy of the original data file.

Introduction **vii**

Topic B: Setting your expectations

Properly setting your expectations is essential to your success. This topic will help you do that by providing:

- Prerequisites for this course
- A description of the target student at whom the course is aimed
- A list of the objectives for the course
- A skills assessment for the course

Course prerequisites

Before taking this course, you should be familiar with personal computers and the use of a keyboard and a mouse. Furthermore, this course assumes that you've completed the following courses or have equivalent experience:

- *Windows 95: Basic* or *Windows 98: Basic or Windows 2000 Basic*

Target student

You should be comfortable using a personal computer and Microsoft Windows 95 or later. You should have little or no experience using Macromedia Dreamweaver 3.0. You should also have little experience in using either Internet Explorer or Netscape to browse the Internet. You'll get the most from this course if your goal is to become proficient using Dreamweaver 3.0 to create Web pages and Web sites and add visual impact to them with colorful text, graphics, links, tables, and frames.

Course objectives

These overall course objectives will give you an idea about what to expect from the course. It is also possible that they will help you see that this course is not the right one for you. If you think you either lack the prerequisite knowledge or already know most of the subject matter to be covered, you should let your instructor know that you think you are misplaced in the class.

After completing this course, you will know how to:

- Understand Basic HTML and Internet concepts, explore and customize the Dreamweaver environment, work with Dreamweaver documents, the HTML Source inspector, and the Quick Tag Editor.
- Create, save and edit documents and enhance documents by setting page properties and insert horizontal rule.
- Format text, insert special characters, paragraph breaks, line breaks, and lists in a document; check spellings in a document and import text into Dreamweaver.
- Plan and define a site, work with the Site window, copy and move site files, set a home page, create a site map, and create, use, and edit templates.
- Link Web pages and differentiate absolute and relative paths, create named anchors and links to the named anchors, create links to Web sites and e-mail addresses.

viii   Dreamweaver 3.0: Basic

- Insert images, modify their alignment, align text around them, and add background images; create links by using an image, image map and text label for an image.

- Add a table, add text to it, add and delete rows and columns, and import tabular data in a Dreamweaver document; insert images in a table, select tables, rows, and columns, format table heading, align text, and modify table properties; change the width, cell spacing, and cell padding of a table, merge cells, and remove table borders; design a Web page by using nested tables and invisible graphics.

- Examine and create a frames page; set frameset and frame properties; create a nested frames page, delete a frame, and create links in a frames page; understand about uploading sites and file naming conventions; check and fix links in a site, upload a site, set download time, and test an uploaded site.

Skills inventory

Use the following form to gauge your skill level entering the class. For each skill listed, rate your familiarity from 1 to 5, with five being the most familiar. *This is not a test.* Rather, it is intended to provide you with an idea of where you're starting from at the beginning of class. If you're wholly unfamiliar with all the skills, you might not be ready for the class. If you think you already understand all of the skills, you might need to move on to the next Module in the series. In either case, you should let your instructor know as soon as possible.

Skill	1	2	3	4	5
Possess Basic Internet and HTML knowledge					
Start and customize Dreamweaver 3.0					
Create, edit, save, and preview documents					
Use the History palette and the Quick Tag Editor					
Enhance documents by setting page properties					
Insert horizontal rule and background colors					
Format documents, insert line and paragraph breaks					
Insert special characters and add lists					
Check spelling and import text					
Plan and create a local site					
Copy and move site files					
Set home page and create site map					
Create, use, and edit templates					
Link pages with a Web site					
Understand absolute and relative links					
Create and use named anchors					
Link to a Web site and an e-mail address					
Add an image and change its alignment					
Add background images					
Create links by using an image					
Create an image map and text label for an image					

x   Dreamweaver 3.0: Basic

Skill	1	2	3	4	5
Add and format a table					
Import tabular data and insert images in a table					
Select tables, rows and columns, format table headings					
Align text in a table and modify table properties					
Change width, cell spacing, and cell padding of a table					
Merge cells in a table and remove table borders					
Design a Web page by using nested tables					
Design a Web page by using invisible graphics					
Examine and create frames					
Set frameset and frame properties					
Create links in frames					
Add nested frames and delete frames					
Check links in a site					
Upload sites and file naming conventions					
Check and fix links in a site					
Upload a site, set download time, and test an uploaded site					

Introduction **xi**

Topic C: Re-keying the course

If you have the proper hardware and software, you can re-key this course after class. This section explains what you'll need in order to do so, and how to do it.

Computer requirements

To re-key this course, your personal computer must have:

- A keyboard and a mouse
- PC with an Intel Pentium processor or equivalent.
- At least 32 MB of RAM.
- 350 MB of available hard disk space.
- A 3 ½ -inch floppy disk drive if you want to load the data files from disk.
- A minimum of a 256-color monitor capable of 800X600 resolution. If a higher resolution is used, some portions of this course will change.
- Internet access if you want to download the data files from the www.courseilt.com Web site and also if you want to do all of the activities in Unit 5, "Connecting Web pages with links."
- An e-mail software configured on the computer if you want to do all of the activities in Unit 5, "Connecting Web pages with links."

Setup instructions to re-key the course

Before you re-key the course, you will need to perform the following steps.

1 Install Windows 98 second edition according to the software manufacturer's instructions. (You can also use Windows 95, if you do, the screen displays might look slightly different than the screen shots in the book.) Ensure that Internet Explorer 5.0 is also installed. Set the home page of Internet Explorer 5.0 to about:blank.

2 Change the display screen area to 800 by 600 pixels.

3 Install Macromedia Dreamweaver 3.0 according to the software manufacturer's instructions. Keep all default settings during installation.

4 Install Netscape Communicator 4.73 according to the software manufacturer's instructions. Do a typical installation. In the Netscape Desktop Preference Options screen, clear Make Netscape Communicator my default Internet Browser option and continue with the installation.

5 Start Netscape Navigator. Once the Creating a New Profile wizard appears, continue to click Next until Set up Outgoing Mail Server dialog box appears. Click Finish to close the dialog box. Netscape Navigator dialog box appears asking whether you would like to register Navigator as your default browser. In the dialog box, check Do not perform the check in the future. Click No to close the dialog box.

6   In Netscape Navigator, choose Edit, Preferences and from the category list, select Navigator. Under Navigator starts with, select Blank page to ensure that the Navigator starts with a blank page every time.

7   Start Dreamweaver 3.0. In the Please Register dialog box, click Don't Remind Me. (To ensure that the Please Register dialog box does not appear every time you start Dreamweaver.)

8   To set Netscape as the secondary browser, in Dreamweaver, choose File, Preview in Browser, and Edit Browser List. Click Plus (+) next to Browsers and in the Add Browser dialog box, click Browse to select the path of Netscape Navigator and click OK. Select NETSCAPE 4.73 and check Secondary Browser.

9   Change the view option in Windows Explorer so that the file extensions are visible. For this, open Windows Explorer. Choose View, Folder Options, and activate the View tab. Under Advanced Settings, clear Hide file extensions for known file types.

10 Install Winzip or comparable file extraction utility to extract data files from zipped files.

11 Download the Student Data examples for the course. You can download the student data directly to student machines, to a central location on your own network, or to a disk.

    1   Connect to www.courseilt.com/instructor_tools.html.

    2   Click the link for Dreamweaver 3.0: Basic.

    3   Follow the instructions that appear on your screen to save the data files.

12 Create a folder called Student Data at the root of the hard drive(C:\.)

13 Extract the zip file for each unit into the Student Data folder. To do so, open the Unit zip file and click the Extract button to display the Extract dialog box. In the Extract To box, type C:\Student Data. Verify that the All Files radio button is selected and the Use Folder Names box is checked; then click the Extract button. The appropriate folder is created with the correct data files in it. For example, after you extract Unit1.zip in the Student Data folder, a Unit1 folder will be created in the Student Data folder that will store all the data files required for Unit1.

14 Ensure that the Document window size of Dreamweaver is set to 583x454 as this is the default Document window size. If this size is not present in the Window Size list, create this window size by choosing Edit Sizes from the Window Size list. Specify 583 as the width and 454 as the height in the Preferences dialog box.

15 If necessary, reset any other defaults that have been changed. In Dreamweaver, palettes that are closed once will not appear when you start Dreamweaver again. The default palettes and inspectors should be reset.

Unit 1

Getting started with Dreamweaver 3.0

Unit time: 40 minutes

Complete this unit and you'll know how to:

A Understand basic Internet and HTML concepts.

B Explore and customize the Dreamweaver environment.

C Work with Dreamweaver documents, the HTML Source inspector, and the Quick Tag Editor.

1–2 Dreamweaver 3.0: Basic

Topic A: Defining the Internet and HTML Basics

Explanation

The Internet has many resources to help you find information you need.

Internet

The *Internet* is an interconnection of several computer networks located all over the world. A *network* is a group of computers linked to each other. Today, networks of universities, businesses, organizations, and governments form the Internet. You can buy music CDs, groceries, and even plan a vacation by using the Internet. The terms Internet and *World Wide Web* (WWW, W3, or Web) are often used interchangeably. However, there are differences between the two.

The Internet refers to the entire network of networks; the Web is just one of the ways in which information is exchanged on the Internet. Computer software applications called *Web browsers* , such as Internet Explorer are used to access *Web sites*. A Web site is a collection of *Web pages*. A Web page (page) is a document that can contain text, graphics, and sound. Web pages are connected by *hyperlinks*. You can move from one page to another by clicking these hyperlinks (links). Hyperlinks help you move through a large document or take you to another Web site. The act of using hyperlinks to move from page to page is known as *browsing* the Web. While browsing the Web, the first page that appears when you access a Web site is called a *home page*.

The Web's easy-to-use system has made it the most popular part of the Internet. The World Wide Web offers several services. These include:

- Electronic mail: *Electronic mail* or *e-mail* is a service on the Internet that allows you to send and receive messages. For instance, the Web site www.hotmail.com allows you to send and receive e-mail messages over the Web.

- Search engines: S*earch engine* is a Web site that helps you to search for information based on a set of specified words. For example, by typing "spice companies in Oregon" in a search engine such as www.yahoo.com, you can find information about several spice companies in Oregon. The search engine will display a list of such companies.

- Electronic commerce: *Electronic commerce* refers to selling and buying products and services on the Web. For instance, you can buy a Philips telephone online from the Web site www.philips.com.

HTML

You create Web pages by using *HyperText Markup Language (HTML)*. HTML is a programming language that contains a series of tags that define the structure of a Web page. An HTML document is a plain text file that contains the HTML code. The name of the file has either .html or .htm extension. You can use a simple text editor, such as Notepad, to create an HTML document.

Do it!

A-1: Some Web concepts

Question	Answer
1 What is the Internet?	
2 What is the difference between the Internet and the World Wide Web?	
3 What is a Web site?	
4 What is a Web page?	
5 What is a hyperlink?	
6 What is a home page?	
7 If you want to find information about different spice companies in Oregon, which service of the Web will you use?	
8 Outlander Spices wants customers to buy spices through its Web site. What type of service is it providing?	

Topic B: Exploring the Dreamweaver 3.0 environment

Explanation

Macromedia Dreamweaver 3.0 is a powerful program that helps you develop dynamic and interactive Web sites. You can easily design, create, and manage Web sites by using Dreamweaver. Most Web sites are created by using HyperText Markup Language (HTML). However, in Dreamweaver, you need not type the HTML code manually. Instead, as you create and design a Web page, Dreamweaver automatically generates its HTML code.

Examining the Dreamweaver environment

By default, the Dreamweaver environment has six components: Document window, Property inspector, Object palette, Launcher, HTML Styles palette, and History palette. You start Dreamweaver by choosing Start, Programs, Macromedia Dreamweaver 3, and Dreamweaver 3.

The Dreamweaver environment is shown in Exhibit 1-1.

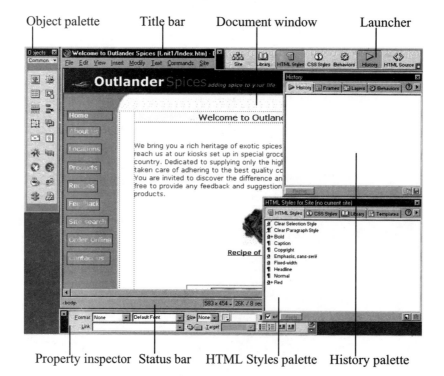

Exhibit 1-1: The Dreamweaver environment

Getting started with Dreamweaver 3.0   **1–5**

The following table describes the components of the Dreamweaver 3.0 environment.

Component	Description
Object palette	Contains icons for objects you can insert into your Web page, such as tables and images. It contains six panels, and each panel contains a group of objects. You can change from one panel to another by selecting the appropriate panel from the pop-up menu at the top of the Object palette. By default, the common panel is selected.
Document window	Displays the current document as you create and edit it. It simulates the current document as it appears in the Web browser. The title bar of the Document window displays the page title, the filename (in parenthesis), and an asterisk if the file contains unsaved changes. It also has the menu bar and the status bar.
Launcher	Contains buttons for opening and closing various palettes, windows and inspectors. You can customize the Launcher according to your needs. The icons on the Launcher are repeated on the Mini-Launcher at the bottom of the Document window. This is done to make access easy when the Launcher is closed.
Property inspector	Displays the most commonly used properties for the selected object. You can see more properties of the selected object by clicking the expander arrow at the lower right corner of the Property inspector.
HTML Styles palette	Creates HTML styles used to apply formatting to a document. An HTML style consists of HTML tags, colors, fonts, and sizes.
History palette	Keeps track of every step of your work in Dreamweaver. It shows a list of all the steps you performed in the active document since you opened or created the document. You can undo and redo a list of actions by using the History palette.

Do it!

B-1: Starting Dreamweaver and identifying components

Here's how	Here's why
1 Choose **Start**, **Programs**, **Macromedia Dreamweaver 3**, **Dreamweaver 3**	To start Dreamweaver.
2 Choose **File**, **Open...**	To display the Open dialog box.
3 From the Look in list, select **Unit1**	(In the Student Data folder.) A list of files appears in this folder. This is the folder you will use in this unit.
Select **Index.htm**	You'll open this file.
Click **Open**	To open the file and close the Open dialog box.

4 Observe the screen	The Dreamweaver environment has six components: Object palette, Document window, History palette, HTML Styles palette, Property inspector, and Launcher. (Refer to Exhibit 1-1.)
5 Observe the Document window	It simulates the current document as it appears in the Web browser.
6 Observe the title bar	The title of the page, "Welcome to Outlander Spices" appears.
7 Observe the menu bar	It has various menu options. You'll use the menu bar options to work with Dreamweaver.
8 Observe the status bar	It contains the HTML tags, Window Size drop down list, the Download Time field, and the Mini-Launcher, which contains the same buttons as the Launcher.
9 Observe the Object palette	It contains icons for objects, such as images, and tables, you can insert into your Web page.
10 Observe the Launcher	It contains buttons for opening and closing inspectors and palettes.
11 Observe the Property inspector	It displays the properties of the selected object. You can examine and edit the properties for the selected object here.

Customizing the Dreamweaver environment

Explanation

The Dreamweaver environment has six components. The most commonly used components are the Document window and the Property inspector. You can customize the Dreamweaver environment according to your needs. You can hide various components of the environment. You can also drag and move various components. To hide a component, choose Window and then the name of the component. To move a component, click and drag the title bar of the component.

Getting started with Dreamweaver 3.0 **1-7**

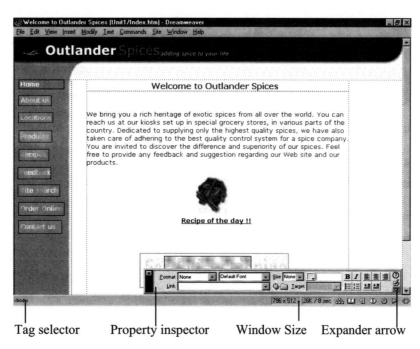

Tag selector   Property inspector   Window Size   Expander arrow

Exhibit 1-2: A customized Dreamweaver environment

Do it!

B-2: Customizing the Dreamweaver environment

Here's how	Here's why
1 Click as shown	To close the Launcher.
2 Choose **Window, Objects**	To close the Object palette.
3 Choose **Window, History**	To close the History palette.
4 Choose **Window, HTML Styles**	To close the HTML Styles palette.
5 Click Maximize	(If necessary. The Maximize button is on title bar of the Document window.) The Document window covers the entire screen.
6 Drag the title bar of the Property inspector so that it is just above the status bar of the Document window	(Refer to Exhibit 1-2.) To move the Property inspector to a desired location.

1–8   Dreamweaver 3.0: Basic

Changing the size of the Document window

Explanation

You might want to view a Web page at a specific size. You can do this by resizing the Document window. You can resize it by using the Maximize button or by dragging the edges or corners of the window. Dreamweaver also provides a quick method, the Window Size pop-up menu, for altering the window size.

To change the size of the Document window, open the Window Size menu from the status bar of the Document window and choose the size you want.

Do it!

B-3:   Resizing the Document window

Here's how	Here's why
1 Click as shown	[796 x 512 | 26K / 8 sec] (On the status bar.) To display the Window Size pop-up menu.
2 From the Window Size pop-up menu, choose **Edit Sizes...**	(To open the Preferences dialog box.) You'll add a new window size to the existing list of window sizes. Note that under the Category list, Status Bar is selected.
3 Under Window Sizes, in the Width column, enter **400**	To specify the width of the window in pixels.
Press (TAB)	To move to the next column.
4 In the Height column, enter **400**	To specify the height of the window.
5 Move to the Description column	Press the Tab key.
In the Description column, enter **My Window Size**	

Width	Height	Description
760	420	(800 x 600, Max...
795	470	(832 x 624, Max...
955	600	(1024 x 768, M...
544	378	(WebTV)
400	400	My Window Size

	To specify a name for the window size.
6 Click **OK**	To close the Preferences dialog box.

Getting started with Dreamweaver 3.0   **1–9**

7 Display the Window Size pop-up menu

Observe the Window Size pop-up menu

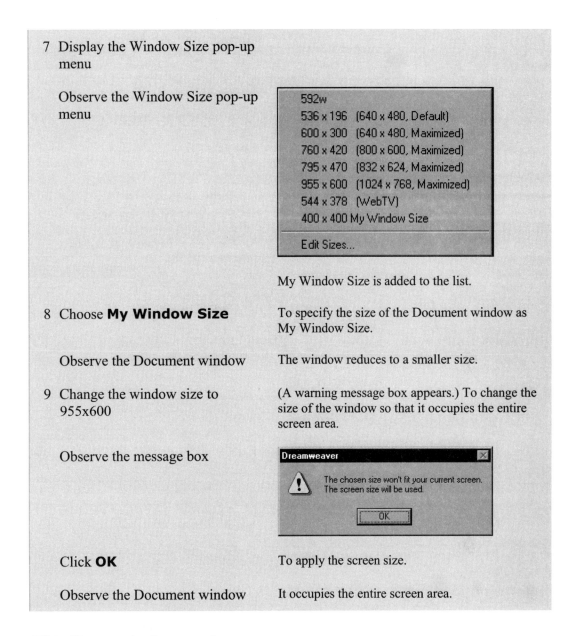

My Window Size is added to the list.

8 Choose **My Window Size**   To specify the size of the Document window as My Window Size.

Observe the Document window   The window reduces to a smaller size.

9 Change the window size to 955x600   (A warning message box appears.) To change the size of the window so that it occupies the entire screen area.

Observe the message box

Click **OK**   To apply the screen size.

Observe the Document window   It occupies the entire screen area.

The Property inspector

Explanation You might want to change the size and format of the text on your Web page. You can do this by using the Property inspector. The Property inspector displays the most commonly used attributes or properties of the selected element. The common properties for text include format attributes such as font size, font type, and alignment. The properties of the Property inspector change depending on the element you select. By default, the Property inspector displays the properties for text on a blank document. You can view more properties by clicking the expander arrow in the lower right corner of the Property inspector.

1–10 Dreamweaver 3.0: Basic

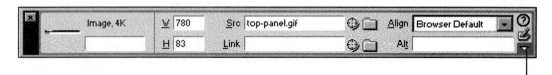

Expander arrow

Exhibit 1-3: The Property inspector showing properties of an image

Do it!

B-4: Examining the Property inspector

Here's how	Here's why
1 Select as shown	You'll examine properties of this image.
Observe the Property inspector	(As shown in Exhibit 1-3.) It displays the commonly used properties of the selected image. Some of the properties are W, H, and Align. These display the width, height, and alignment of the image.
2 Click the expander arrow as shown	To view more properties of the selected image.
Observe the Property inspector	The expander arrow changes to an upper arrow and more properties appear in the Property inspector.
3 Click the expander arrow	To see only the commonly used properties of the selected image.
4 Click at the beginning of the first paragraph	You'll view the properties for this paragraph.
Observe the Property inspector	It displays a set of properties for the first paragraph.

The History palette

Explanation

When you work on a document, you might want to perform an action again or undo a mistake. You can easily undo and redo a list of actions you've performed in the active document by using the History palette. The History palette keeps track of every step of work you've performed in the active document. It has a Replay button that lets you redo actions. The slider, or thumb, points to the last step performed. You can undo a list of actions by using the thumb in the History palette. To display the History palette, choose Window, History.

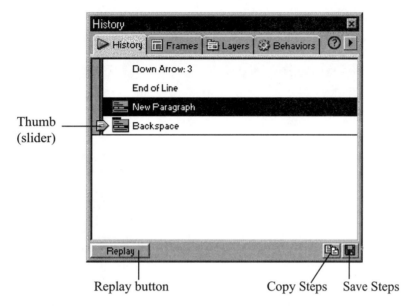

Exhibit 1-4: The History palette

Do it!

B-5: Examining the History palette

Here's how	Here's why
1 Ensure that the insertion point is at the beginning of the first paragraph	You'll examine the History palette.
2 Choose **Window, History**	To open the History palette.
Observe the History palette	It is blank because you have not performed any steps in the active document.
Click the title bar of the History palette	You'll drag the History palette.
Drag the History palette such that it is just above the status bar	

1–12 Dreamweaver 3.0: Basic

3 Press (↓)	To move down in the document.
Observe the History palette	
	It displays the step you've just performed.
4 Press the Down Arrow key two times	
Observe the History palette	
	It displays a count of the number of times you pressed the Down Arrow key.
5 Press (END)	
	It displays the step you've performed.
6 Press (↵ ENTER)	To start a new paragraph.
Observe the History palette	
Observe the document	A new paragraph starts in the document.
7 Press (← BACKSPACE)	To move back to the end of the previous line.
8 In the History palette, select **New Paragraph**	(Refer to Exhibit 1-4.) The Replay button becomes active. You'll replay this step.
9 Click **Replay**	(The Replay button is in the History palette.) To replay the selected step.
Observe the document	A new paragraph is added to the document. Notice that the step is added in the History palette.

Getting started with Dreamweaver 3.0 **1-13**

10	Drag the thumb to Backspace	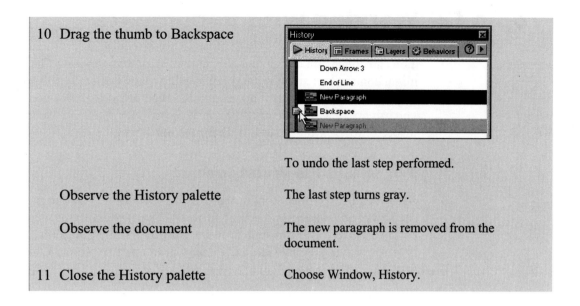
		To undo the last step performed.
	Observe the History palette	The last step turns gray.
	Observe the document	The new paragraph is removed from the document.
11	Close the History palette	Choose Window, History.

Topic C: Working with documents

Explanation

You can create and edit documents in the Document window. The document you create might contain text and objects, such as tables and images. The Document window displays the document as it appears in the Web browser. After you create the document, you can preview the document in the Web browser. You can use the HTML Source inspector to view the HTML code for the document.

Preview in the Web browser

After creating the document in the Document window, you can preview the document to see how it will appear in the Web browser. The appearance of a document differs based on the browser. You can set a browser, such as Internet Explorer, as your default browser. When you preview a document in Internet Explorer, a temporary file is created.

To preview a document in a Web browser:

1. Open the document.
2. Choose File, Preview in Browser.
3. Select the browser in which you want to preview the document.

Exhibit 1-5: A preview of the document in a Web browser

Getting started with Dreamweaver 3.0   **1–15**

Do it!

C-1: Previewing a document in a Web browser

Here's how	Here's why
1 Choose **File**, **Preview in Browser**, **iexplore**	(To preview the document in the Web browser. Maximize the browser window, if necessary.) The Internet Explorer window opens and the document opens in this window.
Observe the title bar of the Internet Explorer window	(Refer to Exhibit 1-5.) The title "Welcome to Outlander Spices" appears in the title bar.
2 Point to the **Products** link	Products
	The pointer changes to a hand, indicating the text is a hyperlink.
Click **Products**	(To view the linked page.) The Products page of the Web site appears in the Web browser.
3 Scroll down the Web page	You can use the scroll bars for scrolling down the Web page to see other contents of the page.
Scroll up the Web page	To go to the top of the page.
4 Click **Back**	(On the Standard toolbar.) To return to the previous page.
5 Click **Forward**	(On the Standard toolbar.) The Products page appears.
6 Close the Web browser	(Choose File, Close.) To return to Dreamweaver.
7 Choose **File**, **Preview in Browser**, **NETSCAPE 4.5**	You'll preview the document in the Netscape browser.
8 Click the **Products** link	To view the Products page.
9 Click **Back**	To return to the previous page.
10 Click **Forward**	To go to the Products page.
Close the Netscape browser	Choose File, Close.

11 Choose **File, Close**	(To close the document.) A message box asking whether you want to save changes in the document appears.
Click **No**	To not save the changes in the document.
Observe the message box	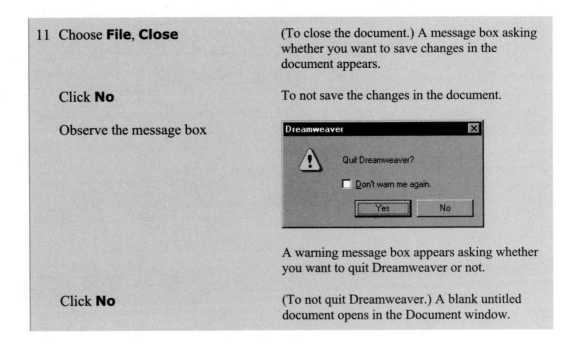 A warning message box appears asking whether you want to quit Dreamweaver or not.
Click **No**	(To not quit Dreamweaver.) A blank untitled document opens in the Document window.

HTML code for a Web page

Explanation   People who have typed their own HTML code to create a Web page can tell you it is a tedious and time consuming process. Fortunately, Dreamweaver takes the headache away by providing a visual interface to create Web pages, eliminating the need to code manually. Instead, you can layout your page by using Dreamweaver, which in turn automatically generates the HTML code that the browser uses to display a document as a Web page.

At times, you will want to look at that code. You can do this by using the HTML Source inspector. You'll notice that any changes you make to the document are immediately reflected in the HTML Source inspector. Any changes made in the HTML Source inspector are updated in the document.

Basic structure of the HTML document

HTML uses *tags* to create the structure of a Web page. Each tag consists of the tag name surrounded by angular brackets as shown here:
    <HTML>

Most of the tags, such as the HEAD tag, work in pairs with a starting and ending tag. These tags are called *containers*. <HEAD> is the *starting* tag and has </HEAD> as the corresponding *ending* tag. The ending tag is identical to the starting tag except that it contains a forward slash (/), as shown here:
    <HEAD>.........</HEAD>

The tags that don't appear in such pairs are called *empty containers*.

A simple page contains the HTML tag, the HEAD tag and the BODY tag. The three basic tags used for creating a simple Web page are:

- HTML: The <HTML> is the starting tag and </HTML> is the ending tag. This tag indicates that the document contains HTML code. An HTML document is divided into two sections- head and body.

- HEAD: The head section of an HTML document starts with the <HEAD> tag and ends with the </HEAD> tag. You can specify the title of the page in this section by using the TITLE tag. The title appears on the title bar of the browser window.
- BODY: The body section starts with the <BODY> tag and ends with the </BODY> tag. This section contains the text that appears in the browser window and other tags in the HTML document.

If you edit the code in HTML Source inspector, you can view the changes in the Document window. To examine the HTML code, choose Window, HTML Source.

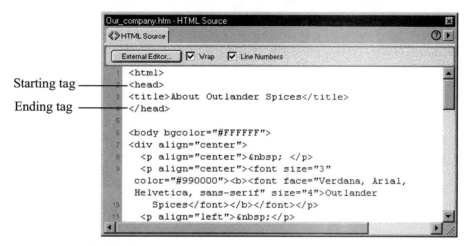

Exhibit 1-6: The HTML Source inspector

Do it!

C-2: Examining the HTML Source inspector

Here's how	Here's why
1 Open Our_company.htm	You'll examine the HTML code of this document.
2 Choose **Window, HTML Source**	To open the HTML Source inspector.
Observe the HTML Source inspector	It displays the HTML code for the Web page.
Drag the HTML Source inspector such that you can see the second paragraph	
3 Check **Wrap**	(In the HTML Source inspector.) The HTML code adjusts according to the width of the HTML Source inspector.
Check **Line Numbers**	(Refer to Exhibit 1-6.) The line numbers appear in the HTML Source inspector.
4 Click in the Document window	To make the Document window active.

5 Select **efficient**	(In the last line of second paragraph.) The text also gets selected in the HTML Source inspector.
Type **competent**	(To replace the text with the new text.) When you add or change content in the Document window, changes are reflected in the HTML Source inspector.
6 In the HTML Source inspector, scroll to the end of the code	To examine the HTML tags.
Observe the </HTML> tag	(The last line of the code.) This tag marks the end of the code for the Web page. The entire HTML code is contained between <HTML> and </HTML> tags.
7 Observe the <HEAD> tags	(You'll have to scroll to the top of the code.) These tags identify the head section of the page.
8 Observe the <TITLE> tags	

```
<head>
<title>About Outlander Spices</title>
</head>
```

	The text within these tags appears on the title bar of the browser window.
9 Observe the <BODY> tags	The ending tag appears at the end of the code. These tags specify the contents of a Web page.
10 Choose **Window, HTML Source**	To close the HTML Source inspector.

The Quick Tag Editor

Explanation

At some point in your Web development, you will want to quickly inspect and edit the HTML source of a single tag within the document. You can use the Quick Tag Editor to do that without switching to the HTML Source inspector. The Quick Tag Editor has three modes: Insert HTML tag, Edit tag, and Wrap tag.

By default, when you open the Quick Tag Editor without selecting anything from the Document window, it opens in the Insert HTML mode. The Quick Tag Editor is used to insert new HTML code. It opens showing a pair of angular brackets with the insertion point between them. You can either select the HTML tag from the list of HTML tags that appear or can enter an HTML tag yourself. If you leave tags unclosed, the corresponding closing tags are added automatically.

If you select some element from the document and open the Quick Tag Editor, it might start in Edit tag mode or Wrap tag mode. If the current selection contains no special formatting, the mode of the Quick Tag Editor is Wrap tag. Otherwise, it opens in Edit tag mode. You can enter only a single opening tag in these two modes.

Getting started with Dreamweaver 3.0   **1–19**

Do it!   **C-3:   Using the Quick Tag Editor**

Here's how	**Here's why**
1 Place the insertion point as shown	 Over the next two years You'll insert HTML tag here.
2 Choose **Modify, Quick Tag Editor**	To open the Quick Tag Editor.
3 Observe the Quick Tag Editor	Insert HTML: <> a abbrev acronym address Over the app we are plann reach out applet mers. We are dreams c area ave a team of au b banner (A list of HTML tags appears.) The Quick Tag Editor opens in Insert Mode.
4 From the list, select **i**	This is the Italics HTML tag.
Press ⏎ *ENTER*	Insert HTML: < i > To insert the tag.
Press ⏎ *ENTER*	To close the Quick Tag Editor.
5 Type **Expansion project**	
Observe the text	*Expansion project* It is italicized.
Open the HTML Source inspector	
Observe the HTML code in the HTML Source inspector	`<i>Expansion project   </i>` (Choose Window, HTML Source.) Remember the HTML Source inspector will display the HTML code based on where the insertion point is in the Document window or what is selected. The opening <I> tag and closing </I> tag are added in the code.
Close the HTML Source inspector	

6	Select as shown	Outlander Spices started its
		You'll wrap the tag for this text.
7	Open the Quick Tag Editor	(Choose Modify, Quick Tag Editor.) It opens in Wrap mode.
	From the list, select **i**	You'll italicize the text.
8	Press (↵ ENTER)	To wrap the tag.
	Press (↵ ENTER)	To close the Quick Tag Editor.
	Deselect and observe the text	Outlander Spices
		It is italicized.
	Open the HTML Source inspector	
	Observe the HTML code in the HTML Source inspector	`<i>Outlander Spices</i>`
	Close the HTML Source inspector	
9	Close the document	Choose File, Close.
	Do not save changes	Click No.
	Click **Yes**	To quit Dreamweaver.

Getting started with Dreamweaver 3.0 **1–21**

Unit summary: Getting started with Dreamweaver 3.0

Topic A   In this unit, you learned about **Internet** and **HTML**. You also defined basic Web concepts.

Topic B   Then, you learned how to **start Dreamweaver**. You explored the **Dreamweaver environment** and identified the various **components** of the Dreamweaver environment. You learned how to **customize the Dreamweaver environment** and **resize the Document window**. You also learned to **examine the Property inspector** and work with the **History palette**.

Topic C   Finally, you learned to **preview a document in the Web browser**. You also learned to work with the **HTML Source inspector** and the **Quick Tag Editor**.

Independent practice activity

1 Start Macromedia Dreamweaver.

2 Open Recipe.htm. (In Unit1 folder under the Student Data folder.)

3 Change the Document window size to 600 X 300.

4 Maximize the Document window.

5 Preview the document in the Web browser.

6 Click the Locations link.

7 Move back to Recipes page.

8 Move forward to Locations page.

9 Close the Web browser.

10 Close the document. (Do not close Dreamweaver.)

11 Open Spice_company.htm.

12 Open HTML Source inspector.

13 View the HTML code of the document.

14 Close the HTML Source inspector.

15 Using the Quick Tag Editor, format "Adding spice to your life" with italic.

16 Close the document. (Do not save the changes.)

17 Close Dreamweaver.

1–22   Dreamweaver 3.0: Basic

Unit 2
Creating Web pages

Unit time: 30 minutes

Complete this unit and you'll know how to:

A Create, save, and edit text in a Dreamweaver document.

B Enhance Dreamweaver documents by setting page properties and inserting a horizontal rule.

2–2 Dreamweaver 3.0: Basic

Topic A: Creating documents

Explanation

As you surf the Web, you'll note that most good Web sites consist of multiple Web pages with a united look and feel. The common features of a site serve a purpose—they make navigation easier, communicate a visual message and differentiate your site from others—but don't need to be complex. Some straightforward formatting and design can readily achieve that common look and feel.

Now, to create one of these well-designed Web sites, you need to start with some planning. Plan what your site is going to look like, how many pages it will have, what's on those pages: content, graphics, and so on. Once you know what you want to create, use Dreamweaver to make your vision a reality.

Adding text

When you start Dreamweaver, a new document opens by default in the Document window. However, you can also create a new document by choosing File, New. You add text to a document by typing as you would in any word processing application. Dreamweaver creates the appropriate HTML tags in the background while you type.

Do it!

A-1: Adding text in a document

Here's how	Here's why
1 Start Dreamweaver	A new document opens by default. You'll add text to this document.
2 Type **Welcome to Outlander Spices**	To enter text in the blank document.
Press ⏎ ENTER	To start a new paragraph.
3 Type the text as shown	Experience our rich exotic spices brought to you from all over the world. You can pick up these spices from our kiosks throughout the country.
4 Start a new paragraph	Press the Enter key.
5 Type **Copyright Outlander Spices 2001-2002. All rights reserved.**	
6 Open the HTML Source inspector	The HTML Source inspector will display the HTML code.
Close the HTML Source inspector	

Creating Web pages **2–3**

Saving documents

Explanation

After adding text to a document, you need to save it for future use. While saving a document, remember to give a meaningful and short name to it. You should not use blank spaces, special characters or punctuation such as colons, periods, or slashes while assigning a file name to a document. Dreamweaver saves files as HTM by default. The .htm extension is added to the document when it is saved. To save the document:

1 Choose File, Save As to open the Save As dialog box.
2 From the Save in list, select the folder where you want to save the document.
3 In the File name box, specify the name of the document.
4 Click Save to save the document.

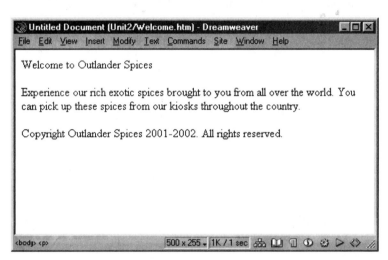

Exhibit 2-1: A sample document

Do it!

A-2: Saving a document

Here's how	Here's why
1 Choose **File**, **Save As**	To open the Save As dialog box.
From the Save in list, select **Unit2**	(In the Student Data folder.) You'll save the document in this folder.
2 Edit the File name box to read **Welcome**	To specify a name for the document. The extension .htm appends to the name of the document.
3 Click **Save**	To save the document.
Observe the title bar of the Document window	The title bar shows Untitled Document followed by the path of the document (as shown in Exhibit 2-1).

2–4 Dreamweaver 3.0: Basic

Editing documents

Explanation

Developing Web pages is a creative process that will require you to review and modify your content to get it just right. As you do so, you will need to add, modify or delete text in the Document window just as you would in a word processing application. After you make the changes, don't forget to save your work.

Do it!

A-3: Editing a document

Here's how	Here's why
1 Place the insertion point after the text **throughout the country.**	throughout the country. You'll add text after this paragraph.
2 Press SPACEBAR	
3 Type the text as shown	Do not hesitate to write us at info@outlanderspices.com
4 Select **write**	Double-click on the word to select it.
5 Type **contact**	Typing replaces selection.
6 Choose **File**, **Save**	To update the document.

Creating Web pages   **2–5**

Topic B: Enhancing documents

Explanation

Dreamweaver offers you a variety of ways to enhance your Web documents. Some of the options include changing the title, altering text color, modifying document margins, adding a background color and background images, or inserting a horizontal rule. Not an exhaustive list, but each of these options will alter the look of your page and make it more appealing.

Adding Colors

Colors can make your web pages more distinctive and eye-catching. For simple colors, such as blue and red, you can assign colors by name in a COLOR attribute of a tag. For more subtle colors, however, you will need to express the attribute value by using its hexadecimal or RGB value, which is represented in the format "#XXXXXX". For specific hexadecimal examples, look at the following table.

Color name	Code
Black	#000000
White	#FFFFFF
Red	#FF0000
Orange	#F87A17
Yellow	#FFFF00
Green	#00FF00
Blue	#0000FF

Fortunately, Dreamweaver makes selecting a color easier than remembering all those hexadecimal codes. In the Page Properties dialog box, click on the down arrow next to a color swatch to display a palette of color choices, and as you do, note that the mouse pointer turns to an eyedropper. When you select a color, the color code is displayed in the corresponding text box.

Page properties

The Page Properties dialog is a central location for specifying a document title, background image, background color, height, and width of a page, as shown in Exhibit 2-2.

Each of these options has a default setting. For example, each new page is untitled unless you assign a title to it. Now, that is different than saving a document with a file name. The title of the document is a descriptive word or group of words that appears in the title bar of the browser window.

2–6 Dreamweaver 3.0: Basic

To set page properties:
1 Choose Modify, Page Properties to open the Page Properties dialog box.
2 In the Title box, enter the title for the page.
3 From the Background list, specify a background color.
4 From the Text list, specify a color for the text.
5 Click OK to apply the settings and close the dialog box.

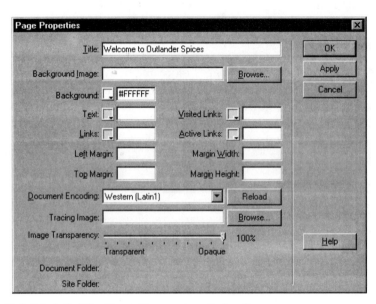

Exhibit 2-2: The Page Properties dialog box

Do it!

B-1: Setting page properties

Here's how	Here's why
1 Choose **Modify**, **Page Properties...**	(To open the Page Properties dialog box.) You'll change the properties of the document.
2 Edit the Title box to read **Welcome to Outlander Spices**	This is the title of the document.
3 Click the down arrow next to Background as shown	A color box appears. Notice that the shape of the pointer changes to an eyedropper.

Creating Web pages **2-7**

4 Select the color as shown		Background: ☐ #FFFFFF (color grid)
		To set the background color for the document.
Observe the Background box		Background: ☐ #CCFFFF
		The color code, #CCFFFF, appears in the box.
5 Click **OK**		To close the Page Properties dialog box.
6 Open Hexcolorchart.htm		(In the Unit2 folder.) This chart contains hexadecimal codes for colors.
Note the color code for blue		
Close the document		
7 Open the Page Properties dialog box		
In the Text box, enter the color code		To set the color for the text in a document.
Close the dialog box		Click OK.
Observe the document		The title of the document, "Welcome to Outlander Spices" appears on the title bar. The background color of the document and the text changes.
8 Update the document		

Horizontal rule

Explanation

A *horizontal rule*, a line that extends across the page, helps in organizing information in a document. You can divide the text and objects, such as images or tables, on a page into different sections by inserting a horizontal rule, as shown in Exhibit 2-3. You can also use the horizontal rule to separate text in the document.

To insert a horizontal rule in a page, place the insertion point where you want to insert the horizontal rule and choose Insert, Horizontal Rule.

2–8   Dreamweaver 3.0: Basic

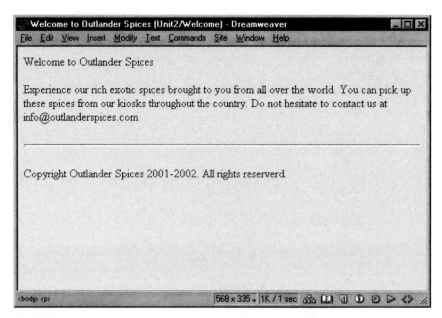

Exhibit 2-3: A horizontal rule in the Welcome document

Do it!

B-2: Inserting a horizontal rule

Here's how	Here's why
1 Place the insertion point after the text info@outlanderspices.com	info@outlanderspices.com You'll insert a horizontal rule here. A horizontal rule is a line that extends across the page.
2 Open the HTML Source inspector	
3 Choose **Insert, Horizontal Rule**	To insert a horizontal rule.
Observe the HTML code in the HTML Source inspector	`<hr>`
Observe the <HR> tag	This tag creates a straight line on a page.
4 Click anywhere on the screen	To deselect the horizontal rule.
Observe the document	The horizontal rule divides the text on a page into two sections, as shown in Exhibit 2-3.
5 Update the document	

Attributes of a horizontal rule

Explanation

Once a horizontal rule has been inserted, you change its appearance by using the Property Inspector as shown in Exhibit 2-4. For instance, you can change the width and height of the horizontal rule to make it appear wider or thicker. The width and height of the horizontal rule can be specified in pixels or as a percentage of the page size. You can also align the horizontal rule to right, left, or center of the document. And last, you can give the rule perspective by checking the Shading box.

In HTML tags, an *attribute* is a named property associated with the tag. Some attributes are necessary while others are optional. The HR tag has many attributes such as WIDTH, SIZE and, NOSHADE. The WIDTH attribute specifies the width of the horizontal rule. The default width is 100%. The SIZE attribute specifies the height of the rule. The NOSHADE attribute specifies that the rule is in a solid color.

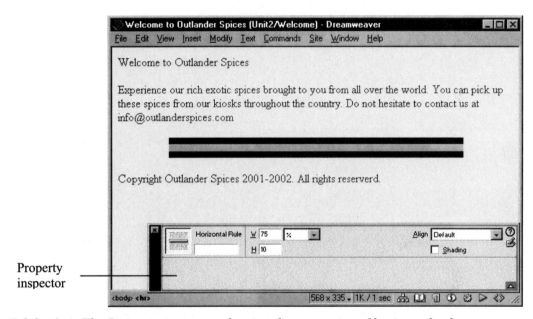

Property inspector

Exhibit 2-4: The Property inspector showing the properties of horizontal rule

Do it!

B-3: Formatting a horizontal rule

Here's how	Here's why
1 Select the horizontal rule	By clicking anywhere on the horizontal rule.
2 Observe the Property inspector	The properties of the horizontal rule appear in the Property inspector.
3 From the W list, select **%** as shown	To specify the width of the horizontal rule in percent.

4 In the W box, enter **75**	To specify the width of the horizontal rule as 75% of the page size.
5 Press (TAB)	
Observe the document	The width of the horizontal rule decreases.
6 In the H box, enter **10**	To specify the height of the horizontal rule in pixels.
7 In the Property inspector, clear **Shading**	To remove shading from the horizontal rule.
Observe the HTML code in the HTML Source inspector	`<hr width="75%" size="10" noshade>`
Observe the \<HR\> tag	The width and size attributes add to the HR tag. The HR tag also specifies that horizontal rule is not shaded.
Close the HTML Source inspector	
8 Deselect the horizontal rule	The height of the horizontal rule increases.
9 Update the document	
10 Preview the document in the Web browser	
Resize the browser window	Click on the Minimize button or drag a Window corner.
Observe the horizontal rule	The width of the horizontal rule has changed to 75% of the window width. Instead of pixels, you set the width of the rule to a percentage, which means that every time a user resizes the window the rule will adjust accordingly.
Close the Web browser	
11 Close the document	Do not quit Dreamweaver.

Unit summary: Creating Web pages

Topic A

In this unit, you learned how to **add text** in a document. You also learned how to **save** and **edit** a document.

Topic B

Finally, you learned how to enhance the appearance of documents by **setting page properties**. You changed the title of a Web page. You also learned to **insert a horizontal rule** on a page and format its width, height, and shading.

Independent practice activity

1 Create a new document.

2 Add text to the document, as shown in Exhibit 2-5.

3 Save the document as **Feedback.htm**.

4 Set the background color of the document to a shade of green.

5 Set the color of the text to a shade of red.

6 Specify the title of the page as **Feedback**.

7 Add a horizontal line after the text, Feedback.

8 Update and close the document.

Feedback

Whether it's the spicy ginger root from the Far East or red chilies grown in Argentina, Outlander Spices offers a complete range of exquisite spices and blends. We deliver the finest imported and domestic spices that are freshly ground in small batches to retain their original flavor.

Help us serve you better by giving us your feedback at getintouch@outlanderspices.com

---

Exhibit 2-5: A sample document after step 2 of Independent practice activity

2–12 Dreamweaver 3.0: Basic

Unit 3
Enhancing documents

Unit time: 30 minutes

Complete this unit and you'll know how to:

A Format text, insert special characters, paragraph breaks, line breaks, and lists in a Dreamweaver document.

B Check the spelling in a Dreamweaver document.

C Import text into Dreamweaver.

3–2 Dreamweaver 3.0: Basic

Topic A: Formatting documents

Explanation

To attract visitors to your site, it is important that your Web pages be well formatted. You can do this by using appropriate font size, color, and face in the document. For example, you can emphasize a paragraph by inserting a descriptive heading and then formatting it with bold and a larger font size. To accomplish this, you select the text, and then using either the Text menu or Property inspector, choose the appropriate formatting.

Font size and color

When formatting text, Dreamweaver offers you a variety of ways to catch a user's attention such as font size and color.

By default, all text is set to the default font size of 3. You can change font size to anything from 1 through 7, each impacting your message in a different way. For example, a small font size of 1 or 2 might be used for a copyright message, because you want it out of the way. Or, you would use a large font size of 5 or 6 to declare emphatically a short message of one or two words, such as "We Won." To set font size; choose Text, Size and then the preferred size number.

When you type in a Dreamweaver document, the color of the text is set to Automatic by default, which is normally displayed as black but will depend upon a user's browser settings. If you want to change the color of the text to a specific color, choose Text, Color and the desired color.

Font face

The font face, such as Arial or Times New Roman, specifies the basic design of text. One limitation of HTML is that you cannot format text with just any font, as you can in a word processing application. That's because users from various platforms, such as Macintosh, Window, and Unix, will be viewing your web pages and they won't all have the same font selection.

A way around this is to format text with a font combination. For example, Arial, Helvetica, sans-serif is one combination. The Web browser uses Arial font, if available. If Arial font is not available the browser uses Helvetica font. If Arial and Helvetica are not available then the browser moves to sans-serif. This ensures that all users will be able to view the text on their computer because it specifies fonts that are installed with the most common browser releases. To set the face of the font, choose Text, Font and the preferred font.

Heading style

Dreamweaver provides six styles of heading, from Heading 1 to Heading 6, that you can apply to text. To specify the heading style, choose Text, Format and the desired heading style.

Nested tags

As you apply multiple formats to text and look at the HTML Source inspector, you will notice the presence of nested tags. What that means is that a tag is opened and closed within another tag. As you look at the following example, note that the bold tag is applied first, but closed last. Within the bold tag, the italic tag is both opened and closed.

```
<b><i>the italic tag is nested within the bold tag</i></b>
```

As a Dreamweaver user, you don't have to think about how or when to nest tags, but it is a good idea to understand how HTML works and what Dreamweaver is doing for you behind the scenes.

Common format tags

While becoming a skilled Dreamweaver user, you will need to be able to identify some of the basic formatting tags. Below is a table listing some of them:

Tag	Type of tag	Description
<B> </B>	Container	Makes text bold.
<I> </I>	Container	Italicizes text.
<U> </U>	Container	Underlines text.
<FONT> </FONT>	Container	Sets the color, face, and size of text on a Web page.
<H1> </H1>	Container	Creates a first level heading.
<P> </P>	Container	Creates a paragraph.
 	Empty	Places text on a new line.

Do it!

A-1: Formatting text

Here's how	Here's why
1 Open About_us.htm	(In the Unit3 folder.) You'll format text in this document.
2 Open the HTML Source inspector	Choose Window, HTML Source.
3 In the Document window, select the text **All spiced up**	
4 Choose **Text**, **Style**, **Bold**	
Observe the HTML Source inspector	`<b>All spiced up</b>`
	The opening and closing tags, <B> and </B>, appear.
5 Choose **Text**, **Style**, **Italic**	To italicize the text.
Observe the HTML Source inspector	`<b><i>About Us</i></b>`
	The opening and closing tags, <I> and </I>, appear. The italics tag is nested within the bold tag.

6	Choose **Text**, **Size**, **5**	To increase the font size of the text.
	Observe the HTML Source inspector	`<font size="5">`All spiced up`</font>`
		The size of the text appears with the opening and closing tags, <FONT> and </FONT>. Remember, the default size is 3.
7	Choose **Text**, **Color...**	(To open the Color dialog box.) You'll change the color of the selected text.
8	Under Basic colors, select a shade of brown	You'll apply this color to the selected text.
	Click **OK**	
	Observe the HTML Source inspector	`<font size="5" color="#800000">`All
		Notice that the code of the color appears.
	In the Document window, deselect the text	The color of the text changes.
9	In the Document window, select the Copyright information	Copyright Outlander Spices 2001-2002. All rights reserved.
10	Choose **Text**, **Font**, **Verdana, Arial, Helvetica, sans-serif**	To change the font of the text.
	Observe the HTML Source inspector	The face of the font changes to the sans-serif font combination.
11	In the Document window, select **About Us**	You'll apply a heading style to this text.
12	Choose **Text**, **Format**, **Heading 1**	To apply Heading 1 to the text.
	Observe the HTML Source inspector	`<h1>`About Us`</h1>`
		The opening and closing tags, <H1> and </H1>, appear.
	Update the document	

Enhancing documents **3–5**

Special characters

Explanation
Dreamweaver provides you with special characters, like the copyright symbol (©) and the registered symbol (®), which you can insert on your Web page. To do so, choose Insert, Characters and then choose the special character that you need.

The following table lists and describes the special characters available in HTML:

Item	Symbol	Description
Copyright	©	Inserts the copyright symbol.
Registered	®	Inserts the registered symbol.
Trademark	™	Inserts the trademark symbol.
Pound	£	Inserts the pound symbol.
Yen	¥	Inserts the yen symbol.
Euro	€	Inserts the euro symbol.
Em-Dash	—	Inserts the em-dash symbol.
Left Quote	'	Inserts the left quote symbol.
Right Quote	'	Inserts the right quote symbol.

Do it!

A-2: Inserting a special character

Here's how	Here's why
1 Select **Copyright**	(At the end of the document.) You'll insert the copyright symbol.
Press (DELETE)	
2 Choose **Insert, Characters, Copyright**	To insert the special character.
Observe the HTML Source inspector	The code for the copyright symbol "©" appears.
Deselect the text	Click anywhere on the document to deselect.
3 Observe the copyright statement	© Outlander Spices 2001-2002. All rights reserved.
	The special character is inserted at the beginning of the last line.
Update the document	

3–6 Dreamweaver 3.0: Basic

Paragraph breaks

Explanation

A large amount of text in one big block is tough to read, especially on a computer screen. You may divide the writing into paragraphs by pressing the Enter key to insert paragraph breaks.

When you press the Enter key, Dreamweaver will add opening and closing paragraph tags to the text. When a browser reads those tags, it will format paragraphs with a blank line between them, separating the blocks of text from each other and making them easier to read.

Do it!

A-3: Inserting a paragraph break

Here's how	Here's why
1 In the Document window, place the insertion point before **Over the next two years**	via the Internet. Over the next two years
2 Press (↵ ENTER)	To insert a paragraph break.
Observe the document	A blank line is inserted between the two paragraphs.
Observe the insertion point in the HTML Source inspector	`<p>over the next two years`
	The opening paragraph tag <P> appears.
3 Press (←)	To move the insertion point to the end of the previous paragraph.
Observe the insertion point in the HTML Source inspector	`via the Internet. </p>`
	The closing paragraph tag </P> appears.

Line breaks

Explanation

You observed in the last activity that a paragraph break inserts a blank line between two paragraphs. But there will be times when you want to start on the line immediately following the break. To do so, you insert a line break by pressing the Shift and Enter keys. Exhibit 3-1 shows an example of where you would insert a paragraph and a line break.

Enhancing documents   **3–7**

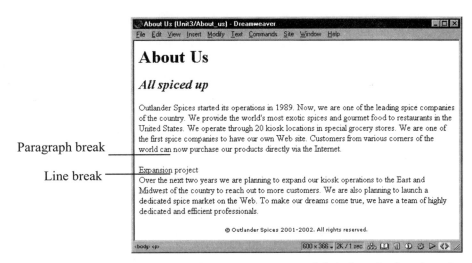

Exhibit 3-1: A sample document showing a paragraph break and a line break

Do it!   **A-4: Inserting a line break**

Here's how	Here's why
1 Place the insertion point before **Over the next two years**	`<p>Over the next two years` In the second paragraph.
2 Type **Expansion project**	You'll insert a line break here.
3 Press SHIFT ⌘ ↵ENTER	To insert a line break.
4 Observe the HTML Source inspector	`Expansion project  ` The line break tag appears. The BR tag does not have a closing tag.
5 Update and close the document	Do not close Dreamweaver.

Formatting paragraphs

Explanation   So far, you've formatted individual words and sentences. In Dreamweaver, as in word processing applications, you can also apply formats to paragraphs, such as alignment and styles.

By default, Dreamweaver aligns all text to the left of the page. You can change that by selecting the paragraph. Next, choose Text, Alignment and then select another alignment, either right or center. You can also set the alignment by using the alignment buttons on the Property inspector.

Another way to format a paragraph is to apply a style. You do this by choosing Text, Format and then by selecting a style, such as Heading 1.

3–8   Dreamweaver 3.0: Basic

Do it!

A-5: Formatting a paragraph

Here's how	Here's why
1 Open Index.htm	You'll format a paragraph in this document.
2 Select the paragraph	We bring you a rich heritage of exotic spices from all over the world. You can reach us at our kiosks set up in special grocery stores, in various parts of the country. Dedicated to supplying only the highest quality spices, we have also taken care of adhering to the best quality control system for a spice company. You are invited to discover the difference and superiority of our spices. Feel free to provide any feedback and suggestion regarding our Web site and our products.
3 Choose **Text**, **Alignment**, **Center**	To center align the paragraph.
4 Observe the HTML Source inspector	`<p align="center">We bring` Notice that the alignment of the paragraph is specified with the paragraph tag.
5 Choose **Text**, **Format**, **Heading 4**	To apply Heading 4 to the entire paragraph.
Observe the HTML Source inspector	`<h4 align="center">We bring` Notice that the heading style is applied to the entire paragraph.
Close the HTML Source inspector	
Deselect the text	The style of the paragraph changes.
6 Update and close the document	Do not close Dreamweaver.

Lists

Explanation

It can be difficult to read paragraph after paragraph on a computer screen. To overcome this, you can vary how information is presented on your Web site, and one way to do that is to use lists. For example, a listing of the world's top 10 companies on a Web page is easier to read than if you were to include them in a paragraph separated only by commas.

In Dreamweaver, you can create three types of lists: ordered, unordered, and definition.

- An ordered list shows items in sequential order. It is also called a numbered list. For example, you can use an ordered list for a recipe page to list the procedures step by step. To create an ordered list, select the text and choose Text, List, Ordered List or use the Property inspector.
- An unordered list is effective for displaying short lines of information. It is also called a bulleted list. To create an unordered list, select the text and choose Text, List, Unordered List or use the Property inspector.

Enhancing documents **3–9**

- A definition list is used to display terms with their definitions. Also called a glossary list, it combines items in pairs. It is usually used for dictionary entries. The first item is the term to be defined and the next line contains the definition.

Exhibit 3-2 shows a definition, an unordered, and an ordered list.

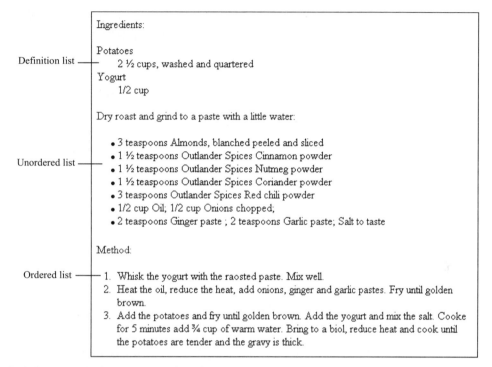

Exhibit 3-2: A document with a definition, unordered, and ordered list

You can change the style of bullets by changing the properties of the list in the Property inspector or by choosing Text, List, Properties.

Do it!

A-6: Adding lists

Here's how	Here's why
1 Open Recipe_1.htm	You'll create ordered and unordered lists in this document.
2 In the Document window, select the text as shown	
	You'll create a definition list.

3 Choose **Text**, **List**, **Definition List**

   Observe the selected text

   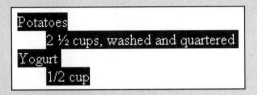

   The text changes to a definition list.

4 Open the HTML Source inspector

   Observe the HTML Source inspector

   The opening tag, <DL>, appears before the definition list. The closing tag, </DL>, appears at the end of the definition list. For every data term, there are corresponding <DT> and </DT> tags. For every definition, there are corresponding <DD> and </DD> tags.

   Close the HTML Source inspector

5 In the Document window, select the text as shown

   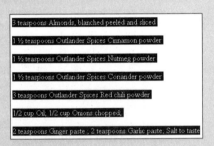

   You'll create an unordered list.

6 Choose **Text**, **List**, **Unordered List**

   Observe the selected text

   The text changes to an unordered list.

7 Open the HTML Source inspector

   Observe the HTML Source inspector

   The opening tag, <UL>, appears before the list. The closing tag, </UL>, appears at the end of the list. For every list item, there are corresponding <LI> and </LI> tags.

   Close the HTML Source inspector

Enhancing documents 3–11

8	In the Document window, select the text under Method	Whisk the yoghurt with the raosted paste. Mix well Heat the oil, reduce the heat, add onions, ginger and garlic pastes Fry until golden brown Add the potatoes and fry until golden brown. Add the yoghurt and mix the salt. Cooke for 5 minutes add ¾ cup of warm water. Bring to a biol, reduce heat and cook until the potatoes are tender and the gravy is thick.
9	Choose **Text**, **List**, **Ordered List**	To create an ordered list.
	Observe the selected text	1. Whisk the yoghurt with the raosted paste. Mix well 2. Heat the oil, reduce the heat, add onions, ginger and garlic pastes. Fry until golden brown. 3. Add the potatoes and fry until golden brown. Add the yoghurt and mix the salt. Cooke for 5 minutes add ¾ cup of warm water. Bring to a biol, reduce heat and cook until the potatoes are tender and the gravy is thick.
		The text changes to an ordered list.
10	Open the HTML Source inspector	
	Observe the HTML Source inspector	The opening tag, <OL>, appears before the list. The closing tag, </OL>, appears at the end of the list. For every list item, there are corresponding <LI> and </LI> tags.
	Close the HTML Source inspector	
11	Deselect the text	
12	In the Document window, place the insertion point as shown	• 3 teaspoons Almonds
		You'll change the bullet style to square.
13	Choose **Text**, **List**, **Properties...**	To open the List Properties dialog box.
14	From the Style list, select **Square**	You'll change the style of bullets to square.
15	Click **OK**	▪ 3 teaspoons Almonds, blanched peeled and sliced ▪ 1 ½ teaspoons Outlander Spices Cinnamon powder ▪ 1 ½ teaspoons Outlander Spices Nutmeg powder ▪ 1 ½ teaspoons Outlander Spices Coriander powder ▪ 3 teaspoons Outlander Spices Red chili powder ▪ 1/2 cup Oil; 1/2 cup Onions chopped; ▪ 2 teaspoons Ginger paste ; 2 teaspoons Garlic paste; Salt to taste
		The square bullets appear.
16	Update the document	

Topic B: Checking the spelling

Explanation

We've all seen professionally published documents--both on the web and in print--that contain spelling mistakes. Our response to them is almost always negative, especially because it is so easy to avoid those errors. That's why you need to use Dreamweaver's Check Spelling feature on all Web documents before posting them on the Internet.

Checking spelling

You can use the Check Spelling dialog box to search the document for spelling errors. As you do so, Dreamweaver will suggest the correct spelling from its dictionary. To open the Check Spelling dialog box, choose Text, Check Spelling.

Once a list of suggestions appears for the incorrect word, all you have to do is select the correct word from the list and click Change. Or, if you have repeated the error, click Change All in the same dialog box to correct all the mistakes. On the other hand, there might be a word that Dreamweaver identifies as misspelled when in fact it is not. You can click Ignore and keep the original word. To keep all instances of the word, click Ignore All.

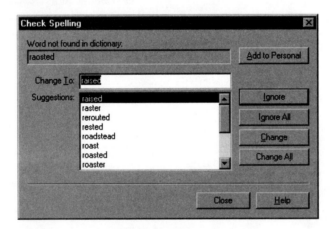

Exhibit 3-3: The Check Spelling dialog box

Enhancing documents **3–13**

Do it!

B-1: Checking the spelling in a document

Here's how	Here's why
1 Choose **Text**, **Check Spelling**	To open the Check Spelling dialog box.
2 Observe the document	The incorrect spelling is highlighted.
Observe the dialog box	Note that the word, "raosted" is selected. A list of suggested alternatives appears in the Suggestions box, as shown in Exhibit 3-3.
3 From the Suggestions list, select **roasted**	To select the correct word. The selected word appears in the Change To box.
4 Click **Change**	To correct the misspelled word in the document. The misspelled word "raosted" changes to "roasted." Now, the word "Cooke" is selected.
5 Correct the spelling to Cook	Select Cook and click Change. Note that the next misspelled word, "biol" is selected.
6 Change the spelling to boil	Now, the word outlanderspices.com is selected.
7 Click **Ignore**	To ignore the word.
Observe the message box	

The message box informs you that the spelling check is complete.

8 Click **OK**	
9 Update and close the document	Do not close Dreamweaver.

3–14 Dreamweaver 3.0: Basic

Topic C: Importing text

Explanation

Many times, creating a Web site requires that you take information from a mixture of sources and transfer it all to Web documents. Dreamweaver makes this easier by offering an assortment of ways to accomplish this task.

Copy and Paste command

To import text, you can open any text editor, such as Notepad or a word processing application, and copy text from it. You then need to use the Paste as Text option in Dreamweaver to paste it in the document. Caution: All the formats will be lost if you copy the text using the Paste option.

To import text:

1 Open the application.
2 Open the file that contains the text.
3 Select the text.
4 Choose Edit, Copy.
5 Activate the Dreamweaver document in which you want to place the text.
6 Place the insertion point in the appropriate location.
7 Choose Edit, Paste as Text.

Do it!

C-1: Importing text using the Copy and Paste commands

Here's how	Here's why
1 Choose **Start, Programs, Accessories, Notepad**	
2 Choose **File, Open...**	
3 Select **Feedback.txt**	In the Unit3 folder.
4 Click **Open**	To open the text file.
5 Choose **Edit, Select All**	To select all the text in the document.
6 Choose **Edit, Copy**	You'll copy the text into a Web document.
7 Close the Notepad window	
8 Verify that the Document window is selected	
Choose **Edit, Paste as Text**	To paste the text in the document without altering the formatting.
9 Save the document as **My_feedback.htm**	
10 Close the document	Do not close Dreamweaver.

Enhancing documents   **3–15**

Open command

Explanation

Suppose you have a collection of favorite recipes stored as text documents and you want to use them for your Web site. A tedious way of reusing the content is with the copy and paste commands, but a simpler way is to use Dreamweaver's Open command. All you have to do is open the file, which was created in a text editor or word processing application, in Dreamweaver and save it as an HTML document.

Here's how:

1   Choose File, Open to display the Open dialog box.
2   From the Files of type list, select the type of document you want to import.
3   Select the file you want to import into Dreamweaver.
4   Click Open.
5   Choose File, Save As to open the Save As dialog box.
6   From the Save as type list, select HTML Documents.
7   Specify a name for the file
8   Click Save.

Do it!

C-2:   Importing text using the Open command

Here's how	Here's why
1 Choose **File, Open...**	
2 From the Files of type list, select **Text Files**	To view the text documents.
3 Select **Feedback.txt**	
4 Click **Open**	The text file opens in Dreamweaver.
5 Save the document as **Feedback.htm**	
6 Close the document	Do not close Dreamweaver.

Importing Word HTML documents

Explanation

Let's say you are creating a Web site and much of the text you want to include already exists in a Word document. The best way to handle this is to convert the Word document to an HTML file. But, when you view the HTML code for this page, you'll see that the tags are complicated. The manual removal of these unwanted tags is difficult, but in Dreamweaver you can use the Clean Up Word HTML feature to remove them.

The Clean Up Word HTML dialog box provides the following options:
- Remove all Word specific markup—removes all Word-specific HTML tags.
- Clean up CSS—removes all Word specific Cascading Style Sheet styles.
- Clean up <font> tags—removes the HTML tags and converts the default text to size 2.
- Fix invalidly nested tags—removes the font markup tags.
- Set background color—helps you to set the background color by entering the hex value.
- Apply source formatting—applies the source formatting options specified in the HTML Format preferences.
- Show log on completion—displays a message box showing the changes made to the document after the clean up.

To import a Word HTML document:
1. Choose File, Import, Import Word HTML to display the Open dialog box.
2. Select the file that you want to import.
3. Click Open to open the Clean Up Word HTML dialog box.
4. Select the required options.
5. Click OK. A message box appears displaying the Clean Up Word HTML results.
6. Click OK.

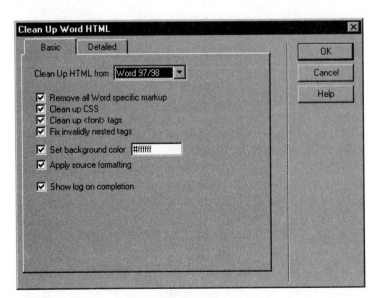

Exhibit 3-4: The Clean Up Word HTML dialog box

Enhancing documents   **3–17**

Do it!   **C-3:   Importing and cleaning up Word HTML documents**

Here's how	Here's why
1 Choose **File, Import, Import Word HTML...**	You'll import a Word HTML document to Dreamweaver.
2 Select **Our_feedback.htm**	
3 Click **Open**	To open the Clean Up Word HTML dialog box, as shown in Exhibit 3-4.
4 Observe the check boxes	Each checked option will determine how the Word file is imported into your Dreamweaver document.
In the Clean Up HTML from list, verify that Word 97/98 is selected	
5 Click **OK**	
	A message box appears displaying the Clean Up Word HTML Results.
6 Click **OK**	To close the message box and the Clean Up Word HTML dialog box.
7 Save the document as **Outlander_feed-back.htm**	
8 Close the document	

Dreamweaver dialog box:

Mon Jun 26 10:49:04 GMT+0530 (India Standard Time) 2000

Clean Up Word HTML Results:
2 Meta Tags Removed
Background Color Set to #ffffff
Source Formatting Applied

OK

3–18 Dreamweaver 3.0: Basic

Unit summary: Enhancing documents

Topic A In this unit, you learned how to **format text** and **insert special characters** in a document. You learned how to add **definition, ordered,** and **unordered lists.** You also learned to insert **paragraph breaks** and **line breaks** and how to **format paragraphs**.

Topic B Next, you learned to **check the spelling** in a document using the Check Spelling dialog box.

Topic C Finally, you learned to import text using the **Copy** and **Paste as Text** commands and by using the **Open** dialog box. You also learned to **import and clean up Word HTML documents**.

Independent practice activity

1 Open Recipe_3.htm.

2 Format the text "Chicken stuffed with spices" as **Heading 2**. Center the text and apply a shade of blue color.

3 Select copyright and replace it with the copyright character.

4 Create an unordered list in the document as shown in Exhibit 3-5.

5 Create an ordered list in the document, as shown in Exhibit 3-6.

6 Correct the spelling errors in the document.

7 Update the document.

8 Close the document.

9 Open Products.txt in Notepad. Copy all the text, and then in a blank Dreamweaver document, paste it as text.

10 Save the document as **Products.htm**.

11 Close the document.

12 Import and clean the Word HTML document Our_products.htm in Dreamweaver using the default options.

13 Save the document as **My_products.htm**.

14 Close the document.

Enhancing documents   **3–19**

For the stuffing:

- 4 **Outlander Spices** Cloves
- 2 **Outlander Spices** Cinnamon sticks, 1" each
- 2 **Outlander Spices** cardamoms
- 2 **Outlander Spices** Bay leaves
- 3 teaspoons **Outlander Spices** Ginger powder
- 10 Cashew nuts, ground to a paste with a little water
- 2 teaspoons **Outlander Spices** Coriander powder
- 0.28 ounces Almonds, blanched, peeled and sliced
- 0.42 ounces Sultanas/Raisins, chopped
- 0.63 pints/2 tablespoon Oil; 2 Onions, sliced; Salt to taste

For the chicken:

- 0.21 pints Clarified butter/refined oil
- 2 teaspoons **Outlander Spices** Garlic powder
- 2 teaspoons **Outlander Spices** Ginger powder
- 0.63 pints Milk
- 0.63 pints Yogurt
- 8 Onions, sliced; Salt to taste

Exhibit 3-5: The Recipe_3 document after step 4 of the Independent practice activity

---

Method:

1. Heat the oil for the stuffing. Add the cloves, cinnamons, cardamoms, and bay leaves. Remove from the oil and grind together with a little water. Keep aside.
2. Add the ginger and cashew nut paste. Add the coriaander powder and salt. Sauté until light brown in color.
3. Add the sliced almonds and sultanas. Stir and add the ground spices and ground onions. Stir well.
4. Remove the pan from the heat and stuff the chiken with the mixture. Close the cavity with cocktail sticks. Lace the chicken with string, so that it does not lose shape and holds in the stuffing.
5. Heat the oil for the chicken in a large pan. Add the sliced onions and fry until transparent; then add ginger and garlic. Fry until the water has evaporated. Add the chicken and fry carrfully, browning it all over. Put in salt and milk. Bring to a boil. Simmer, keeping the pan covered, until the chicken becomes very tender and a little gravy is left. Whisk and add the yogurt to the gravy, stir and put on very low heat until the gravy is thick.

Exhibit 3-6: The Recipe_3 document after step 5 of the Independent practice activity

3–20 Dreamweaver 3.0: Basic

Unit 4

Designing a site

Unit time: 50 minutes

Complete this unit and you'll know how to:

A Plan and define a local site.

B Work with the Site window, and copy and move site files.

C Set a home page and create a site map.

D Create, use, and edit templates.

4–2 Dreamweaver 3.0: Basic

Topic A: Creating sites

Explanation

The first step in creating a Web site is planning. You should plan both the design and content of the site. This may seem basic, but it will save you significant time and effort later on. Once you're ready to start designing your Web site, you'll create a local site on your computer. This is where you'll do the actual work through the various drafts and testing of your site before posting it on the Internet.

Planning a site

Before you create a site, the first step is to plan its structure. You need to decide the folder hierarchy you will use for the site and the files that will be stored in each folder. It is a good practice to store Web pages and images in separate folders. You also need to plan the:

- Navigation of the site
- Templates for the site

You should keep the target audience in mind while designing the site's navigation. The site must have a simple and clear way to access the information on the site. It should be easy for the visitors to know, all the time, where they are in the site.

You also need to plan the *templates* for the site. Templates are pre-designed Web pages you can use to give a consistent appearance and structure to the site. Another advantage of templates is that if you want to change the layout of the pages, you just need to change it in the template and all the pages will be automatically updated with the new layout.

Since a Web site usually includes lots of information, it is necessary to organize and divide the information into smaller chunks on separate pages. To do this, all files for the Web site must be stored in the same folder. After you have created the Web pages, you put them together to create a Web site.

Local site

As you begin your Web site, you'll be creating a *local site* on your computer with a name and a local root folder to store all the files of the site. This is where you'll keep your work in progress before posting it on the Internet. When declaring the site's root folder, make sure not to use the hard disk or the Dreamweaver application folder.

While defining a site, you'll notice the HTTP Address option at the bottom of the Site Definition dialog box. Once you are ready to post your site on the Web, you will have to secure your *URL (Uniform Resource Locator)*. The URL is your site's address on the Web, such as http://www.outlanderspices.com. You also need an account for your site with an ISP (Internet Service Provider) or Web server. You'll learn about all of these in later units.

To define a local site:

1 Choose Site, New Site to open the Site Definition dialog box.
2 Under Category, verify that Local Info is selected.
3 In the Site Name box, specify the site name.
4 In the Local Root Folder box, specify the local root folder.
5 Click OK to create the site.

Cache file

You must have noticed that when you access a Web site for the first time, it takes some time to open the site. But when you return to a page you've recently looked at, the page opens quickly because the browser has stored the temporary location on the computer. This temporary location is the *cache file*. A cache file helps the browser to open Web pages quickly. Therefore, when you create a site, Dreamweaver prompts you to create a cache file for the site.

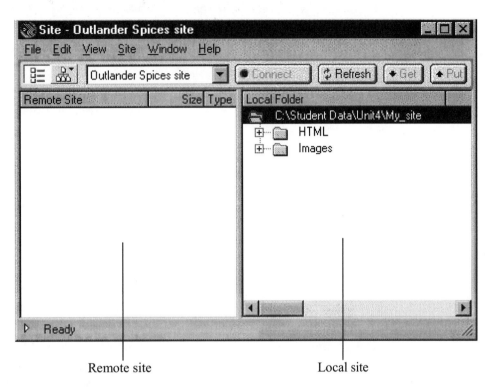

Exhibit 4-1: The Site window

4–4 Dreamweaver 3.0: Basic

Do it!

A-1: Defining a local site

Here's how	Here's why
1 Choose **Site, New Site...**	(To open the Site Definition dialog box.) You'll create a new site. Note that from the Category list, Local Info is selected.
2 Edit the Site Name box to read **Outlander Spices site**	To specify the name for the site.
3 Click the folder icon as shown	Local Root Folder: C:\
	(The Choose Local Folder dialog box appears.) You'll select the root folder where you'll store all the files of the site.
Select **My_site**	In the Unit4 folder.
Click **Open**	(To open the root folder for the site.) The two subfolders HTML and Images are visible.
4 Click **Select**	(To select the root folder.) Note that the entire path of the selected folder appears in the Local Root Folder box.
5 Click **OK**	A message box appears asking you whether you want to create a cache file for the site.
6 Click **Create**	To create a cache file for the site.
Observe the message box	Scanning all files in site — Scanned 4 of 14 — /HTML/Location.htm — Stop
	It shows the progress in saving the cache file on the hard disk. The Site window appears (refer to Exhibit 4-1).

Designing a site   **4–5**

Topic B: Working with the Site window

Explanation

After you have created a site, you might want to rearrange its pages. You can easily do so by using the Site window. You can also use the Site window for standard file maintenance, such as creating new HTML documents, moving files, creating folders, and deleting *site elements*. A site element is a file or a folder in the root folder of the site.

The Site window

The Site window displays the site file structure much like Windows Explorer does. As you look at the Site window as shown in Exhibit 4-2, you'll notice that by default it is divided into two panes—on the right, the local site is displayed, and on the left are the *remote site* files. A remote site is where your site will be posted on the Internet. Its location, which we'll discuss in a later unit, will depend on your situation and could be on a remote server, a local network or your own computer. But for now, it is important to note that you can use the Site window to transfer files between local and remote sites.

Since the remote site does not exist at the moment, you can hide the left pane. To do so, use the View toggle button at the bottom left of the window.

Images

Images and graphics are an effective way of communicating with visitors to the site. You can enhance the appearance of Web pages by using images, about which you'll learn more later.

Hyperlinks

While viewing a Web page on the Internet, you often come across words that are underlined. These are *hyperlinks*, or links, and when you click on them they display a different page. The Web pages of a site are often linked to each other using hyperlinks to make navigation easy.

4–6 Dreamweaver 3.0: Basic

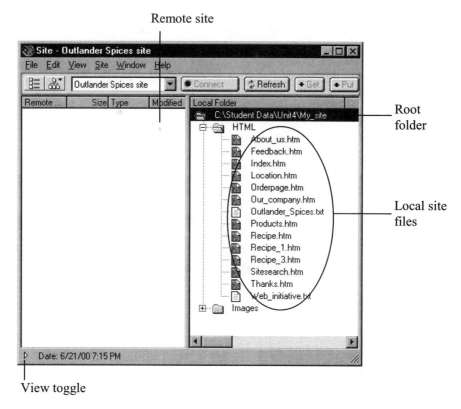

Exhibit 4-2: The Site window displaying local site files

Do it! **B-1: Examining the Site window**

Here's how	Here's why
1 Observe the Site window	The right pane of the Site window displays the root folder for the site My site. It stores all the folders and files needed for the local site. The left pane displays the remote site files. It is empty because Dreamweaver is not connected to a service provider.
2 Click ▷	(The View toggle is located on the left side of the status bar of the Site window.) To hide the left pane of the Site window.
3 Click ◁	To display the left pane.
4 In the right pane, click the plus (+) sign as shown	To view the contents of the Images folder.

5 In the right pane, click the minus (–) sign as shown

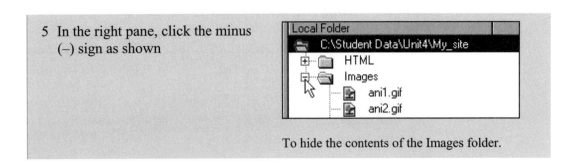

To hide the contents of the Images folder.

Copying site files

Explanation

You might need to copy some site files from one location to another. For instance, you might want to copy an image to your Web pages. You can use the Site window to copy site files to a document and to copy files from one folder to another.

To copy a site file to a document:

1. In the Site window, double-click the document to open it.
2. Restore the Site window.
3. Resize the Document window so that both the Document and the Site window are visible.
4. In the Site window, select the file you want to copy.
5. Drag the file from the Site window to the Document window to copy the file.

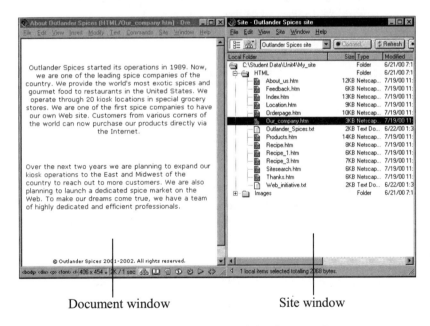

Exhibit 4-3: The Document window and the Site window

4–8   Dreamweaver 3.0: Basic

Do it!

B-2:   Copying site files to a document

Here's how	Here's why
1 Hide the left pane of the Site window	Click the View toggle.
Expand the HTML folder	(Click the plus (+) sign next to the HTML folder.) To display all the files in this folder.
2 Double-click **Our_company.htm**	To open the document in the Document window.
3 View the Site window	If necessary.
4 Resize the Document window and the Site window	(As shown in Exhibit 4-3.) You'll copy the image file from the Site window to the Document window.
5 In the Site window, expand the Images folder	To display the contents of this folder.
6 Select **Logo.gif**	You'll copy this image file to the Document window.
7 Drag Logo.gif from the Site window to the top of the document in the Document window	About Outlander Spices [HTML/Our_company] - Dreamweaver File Edit View Insert Modify Text Commands Site Window He Outlander Spices started its operations in 1989. Now, To copy the image file from the Site window to the Document window.
8 Update and close the document	Do not close the Site window.

Moving site files

Explanation

It is a good practice to keep similar files together in a folder, because it helps in organizing your site. You can move files into a new folder or to an existing one. When you move a file, Dreamweaver automatically checks the hyperlinks on the page and prompts you to update them.

To create a new folder in the Site window, select the root folder and choose File, New Folder. Type the name for the folder and press Enter.

To move site elements into a folder, select the file and drag it into the new folder location. When prompted, click Update to change the links.

To move site elements to a new folder:

1   In the Site window, select the root folder.

2   Choose File, New Folder to create a new folder.

3   Specify a name for the folder.

4   Select the file you want to move and drag it to the folder to which you want to move the file.

5   Update the links if needed.

Designing a site   **4–9**

Do it!   **B-3:   Moving site files to a new folder**

Here's how	Here's why
1 View the Site window	
2 Hide contents of the HTML and the Images folder	Scroll up, if necessary.
Select **My_site**	This is the root folder. You'll create a new folder under this folder.
3 Choose **File**, **New Folder**	(In the Site window.) To create a new folder.
Enter **Text_docs**	To specify the name of the newly created folder.
Press ⏎ ENTER	To create the folder Text_docs. You'll move site files into this folder.
4 Expand the HTML folder	⟨
5 Select **Outlander_Spices.txt**	Our_company.htm Outlander_Spices.txt Products.htm Recipe.htm (Scroll up, if necessary.) You'll move this text file to the Text_docs folder.
Drag the file and drop it to the Text_docs folder	Update Files Update links in the following files? Update /Text_docs/Outlander_Spices.txt Don't Update Help A dialog box appears asking whether you want to update links in the file. A link is the path to a file.
Click **Update**	To update the links in the file.
In the Site window, observe the contents of the Text_docs folder	Text_docs Outlander_Spices.txt The file Outlander_Spices.txt is moved to this folder.
6 Move Web_initiative.txt to the Text_docs folder	Select the file and drag it to the folder and drop it. Click Update when asked to update the links.

4–10 Dreamweaver 3.0: Basic

Topic C: Working with site maps

Explanation

You can use a site map to graphically show the structure of the Web site. The site map is like a business organization chart. It helps you to know how the information is organized on the Web site. You can also use the site map to view the local site and add or modify files. Links can also be removed by using the site map. But, before creating a site map, you need to set a *home page* for the site.

Home page for the site

When you type an address in your Web browser, such as www.outlanderspices.com, the first page that is displayed is the home page. A well-designed site will include a home page that provides a welcome statement and an overview of the Web site's contents. You then click on links to view other pages containing more specific information.

By default, your browser first tries to find a file by the name of Index.htm or Index.html and gives an error message if the file is not found. That is why you name the home page as such, and use Dreamweaver's Site window to define which file is the home page.

To set a home page, in the Site window, select the Web page to be set as the home page and choose Site, Set as Home Page.

Do it!

C-1: Setting a home page for the site

Here's how	Here's why
1 Expand the HTML folder	If necessary.
2 Select **Index.htm**	You'll set this document as the home page for the site.
3 Choose **Site**, **Set as Home Page**	
4 Preview the document in the Web browser	(In the Site window, choose File, Preview in Browser, iexplore.) To view the home page in the Web browser.
Close the Web browser	

Creating a site map

Explanation

The site map shows the hierarchy of your Web site and gives a visual representation of the site structure. It shows HTML files as icons and the home page as the starting point of the map. It also shows how the files are linked in the site. You can show or hide pages in the site map by clicking the plus (+) or minus (-) sign next to the page in the map. Some files, like the image files and templates, do not appear in the site map and are called *dependent files*. The layout of the site map can be modified according to your requirements. The site map can also be used to add new files to the site and to add, remove, and modify links.

You can create a site map by choosing Window, Site Map.

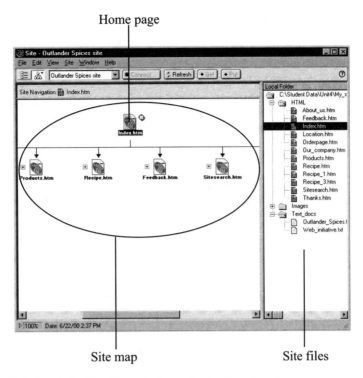

Exhibit 4-4: The Site window displaying the site map

Do it!

C-2: Creating a site map

Here's how	Here's why
1 Verify that the left pane of the Site window is visible	Click the View toggle.
2 Choose **Window, Site Map**	(To create the site map.) Note that a message box appears on the screen informing you that Dreamweaver is building the site map.
3 Observe the Site window	The left pane of the Site window shows the site map as shown in Exhibit 4-4. The site map shows the hierarchy of the Web site with the home page on the top.
4 Click the plus sign next to Products.htm	To view all the documents to which this document is linked.
5 Close the Site window	

4-12 Dreamweaver 3.0: Basic

Topic D: Working with templates

Explanation

A Web site looks better if it has Web pages with a common structure and appearance. As you know, there can be any number of Web pages in a site. Creating a layout for each page of the site could be tedious. Instead, you can create a template with the desired layout and then base all the Web pages on it. Once you base your Web pages on a template, modifying the layout of all the Web pages by changing the template is much easier and less time-consuming than changing each individual page.

Creating templates

Before you start creating a template, you need to decide on the content that should be the same for all pages and the content that will vary from page to page.

A template has two regions, *editable* and *locked*. The contents of an editable region can be changed and the contents of the locked cannot. For example, the text that varies from page to page can be put in the editable region while the company logo and copyright information would be in a locked region. To indicate the style and location of the content of individual pages, you can use the placeholder text and define it as an editable region. You can also specify the background color and the format of the text in the template.

By default, when you save the template, all the regions on it are marked as locked. To make a template useful, you must make some parts of it editable. While editing a template, you can make changes to both editable and locked regions. But when the template is applied to a document, or when you create a new document based on the template, you can only make changes to the editable region. Dreamweaver automatically creates a Templates folder in the root folder of the site to store all the templates of the site.

To create a template:

1 Open a blank document.
2 Type the content of the locked region and format it the way you want.
3 Set the page properties, if needed.
4 Choose File, Save as Template to open the Save As Template dialog box.
5 Specify the name of the template and click Save to save the template.
6 Choose Modify, Templates, New Editable Region and specify the name for the editable region.
7 Apply a format of your choice to the editable region.
8 Update and close the template.

Designing a site **4–13**

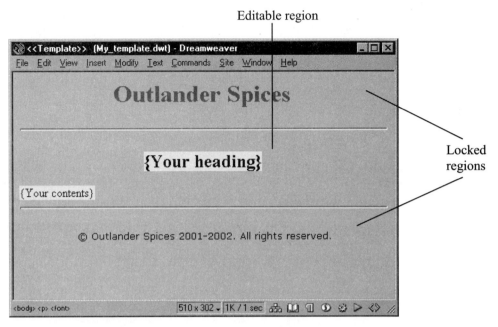

Exhibit 4-5: A template showing the editable and locked region

Do it! **D-1: Creating a template**

Here's how	Here's why
1 Verify a blank page is open in the Document window	
2 Choose **Modify**, **Page Properties...**	
3 Edit the Title box to read **The spice company**	
Set a gray color as the Background color	Click the Background list and select a gray color.
4 Click **OK**	
5 Type **Outlander Spices**	This is a heading in the template.
Change the format of Outlander Spices to Heading 1	Choose Text, Format, Heading 1.
Align the text to the center	Choose Text, Alignment, Center.

	Set a red color as the font color	Choose Text, Color, select a red color, and click OK.
	Deselect the text	
6	Insert a horizontal rule	(Below the text.) Choose Insert, Horizontal Rule.
7	Choose **File**, **Save as Template...**	To open the Save As Template dialog box.
	Verify that from the Site list, Outlander Spices site is selected	To create a template in this site.
	Edit the Save As box to read **My_template**	
		To specify the name of the template.
8	Click **Save**	The name of the template appears in parentheses with .dwt extension on the title bar.
9	Deselect the horizontal rule	(Click at the end of the horizontal rule.) You'll create an editable region.
10	Press `← ENTER`	To insert a new paragraph in the template.
11	Choose **Modify**, **Templates**, **New Editable Region...**	(To open the New Editable Region dialog box.) You'll create an editable region in the template.
	In the Name box, enter **Your heading**	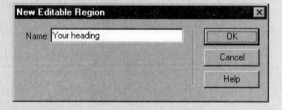
		To specify a placeholder text for the editable region.
	Click **OK**	
	Observe the Document window	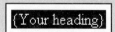
		The text "Your heading" appears in braces and is highlighted.

Designing a site   **4-15**

12	Change the format of Your heading to Heading 2	You'll use this region for the second heading of the document.
	Align the text to the center	
	Deselect the text	
13	Press ⏎ ENTER	To insert a new paragraph in the template.
14	Insert another editable region	Choose Modify, Templates, New Editable Region.
	Specify the placeholder text as **Your contents**	In the Name box, enter Your contents and click OK.
15	Change the format of Your contents region to None	(Choose Text, Format, None.) To remove formatting for this editable region. Note that Your contents editable region is left aligned.
	Deselect the text	
16	Press ⏎ ENTER	To insert a new paragraph in the template.
17	Insert a horizontal rule	
	Deselect the horizontal rule	
18	Type the copyright information as shown and center it	© Outlander Spices 2001-2002. All rights reserved.
	Set the font of the text you just typed to Verdana, Arial, Helvetica, sans-serif	
	Observe the text you just typed	You'll not be able to edit this copyright information when you create a document using this template.
19	Update and close the template	Do not close Dreamweaver.

Using templates

Explanation

Once the template is created, you can use it to create new documents or apply it to an existing document. When you create a document based on a template, you can only make changes to the editable region; the locked region remains unchanged.

To create a document by using a template:

1   Choose File, New from Template.
2   Select the template you want to use.
3   Select the editable region and type the content.
4   Save the document.

4–16 Dreamweaver 3.0: Basic

Do it!

D-2: Creating a document by using a template

Here's how	Here's why
1 Choose **File**, **New from Template...**	(To open the Select Template dialog box.) To create a document based on a template. Note that from the Site list, Outlander Spices is selected.
2 From the Templates list, select **My_template**	
Click **Select**	To base the document on the template.
3 Select **{Your heading}**	You'll edit this text.
Type **Adding spice to your life**	This is the second heading for the document.
4 Open About_us.txt	(Open this file in Notepad. It is in the Unit4 folder.) You'll copy text from this file.
Select and copy the text	Choose Edit, Select All to select the text and Edit, Copy to copy it.
Close Notepad	
5 Activate the Dreamweaver environment	
Select **{Your contents}**	You'll edit this text.
Choose **Edit**, **Paste as Text**	
6 Save the file as **My_document.htm**	In the My_site folder.
7 Preview the document in the Web browser	
Close the Web browser window and the document	Do not close Dreamweaver.

Editing templates

Explanation

You might want to modify the design of the pages based on templates. For this, you do not need to make changes to each page of the site. Changes can be reflected in all the pages by editing the template. Dreamweaver asks you to update only the pages that use the template.

To edit a template:

1. Open the template in the Document window.
2. Make the changes that you want in the template.
3. Update the template and the Update Pages dialog box appears.
4. Click Update to update the document based on the template.

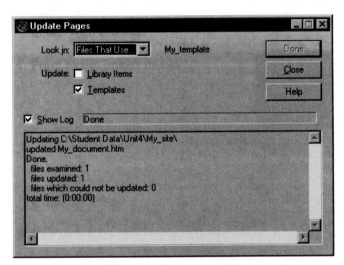

Exhibit 4-6: The Update Pages dialog box

4–18 Dreamweaver 3.0: Basic

Do it!

D-3:   Editing a template

Here's how	Here's why
1 Choose **File**, **Open...**	To display the Open dialog box.
From the Files of type list, select **Templates Files**	To view template files.
Select **My_template.dwt**	In the Templates folder under the My_site folder.
Click **Open**	
2 Select the Your heading editable region and italicize it	You'll change the format of this region.
Deselect the editable region	
3 Set a light pink color as the Background color of the template	
4 Update the template	

	A message box appears asking whether to update the template files used in the files.
Click **Update**	The Update Pages dialog box appears as in Exhibit 4-6 showing the number of files examined and updated.
Click **Close**	
5 Close the template	Do not close Dreamweaver.
6 Open My_document.htm	You'll check whether the document is updated with the changes in the template.
Observe the document	It has a pink background color and the sub heading is italicized.
Close the document	Do not close Dreamweaver.

Designing a site **4-19**

Unit summary: Designing a site

Topic A   In this unit, you learned how to **plan a site** and **create a local site**.

Topic B   Then, you learned about the **Site window**. You also learned how to **copy site files** to a document and to **move site files** to a folder.

Topic C   Next, you learned how to **set a home page** and **create a site map**.

Topic D   Finally, you learned how to **create**, **use**, **and edit a template**.

Independent practice activity

1   Create a site with the name, **Practice site**. (Use Unit4ipa under Unit4 as the root folder. It has all the files needed for the site.)

2   Open Princely_potatoes.htm and copy rec2.jpg from the Site window to the beginning of the document. (The jpg file is in the Images folder under the root folder). Save and close the file.

3   Under the Unit4ipa root folder, create a new folder by the name **Text_files** and move all the text files from the HTML folder to this folder. Update the file links.

4   Set Index.htm as the home page for the site.

5   Create a site map for the site.

6   Close the Site window.

7   Create a template as shown in Exhibit 4-7. Set the font of the copyright information as Verdana and font size as 1.

8   Save the template as **Spice_template** in the Practice site.

9   Create an editable region with the name **Contents,** as shown in Exhibit 4-7.

10 Set the font for the Contents region as Verdana and font size as 2.

11 Update and close the template.

12 Create a document based on Spice_template. Open Our_spices.txt in Notepad and copy and paste the text in the Contents editable region of the document. (The text file is in the Unit4ipa folder.)

13 Save the document as **Spice_document.htm**. (In the Unit4ipa folder.) Compare your work with Exhibit 4-8.

14 Preview the document in the Web browser.

15 Close the Web browser and the document. Close Notepad.

Exhibit 4-7: The template after step 11 of the Independent practice activity

Exhibit 4-8: The Spice_document after step 12 of the Independent practice activity

Unit 5

Connecting Web pages

Unit time: 40 minutes

Complete this unit and you'll know how to:

A Link Web pages and distinguish absolute from relative paths.

B Create named anchors and links to the named anchors.

C Create links to Web sites and e-mail addresses.

Topic A: Linking pages

Explanation

Surfing the Internet, you often come across blue, underlined words that are called *text hyperlinks* or simply *links*. When you click a link, your browser will perform an action. The browser action depends upon what the link is supposed to do, such as display a different Web page, move to a particular portion of a Web page, download a file, open an application, compose an e-mail to a specific address, or access a newsgroup.

The most common use of links is to display a different page and is frequently used to organize a Web site across many pages. For example, you visit www.msn.com and the browser displays the home page. All of the site information is not on that one page. You read what the home page says and navigate to another page for more specific information by clicking a link.

As you may have noticed while surfing, you can also use an image or an object to accomplish the same result.

Linking to another Web page

Most Web sites will not place all information on a single page. It is just not a prudent way to attract users and have them come back again and again. That means you need to design your Web site with multiple pages in mind. For instance, on the Outlander Spices home page, you can give a brief description about products and then create a hyperlink to the products page. The user can click the hyperlink for more information about the products.

A text hyperlink is generally blue and underlined. When you point to it, the pointer changes to a hand as shown in Exhibit 5-1, and the link's address appears on the status bar of the browser. Clicking the hyperlink displays the linked page in the browser. There are many ways to create text links, such as using the menu option, typing the file name in the Link box of the Property inspector, and using the drag and drop method. First, you'll learn how to use the menu option to create links.

The A tags

The Anchor or A tag is used to create a hyperlink. For example,
```
<a href="home.htm">Home</a>
```

In this HTML code, a browser will display the text "Home," between the A tags, as normal text with two additional formats, blue and underlined. When you click this text, the browser will display the home page. The HREF attribute of the A tag is used to specify the Web resource to which the hyperlink links. NAME is another attribute of the A tag that is used to specify a unique name for the anchor. This name is used in specifying it as a destination of another link.

To create a hyperlink using the menu option:

1   Select the text on which you want to create the hyperlink.
2   Choose Modify, Make Link to open the Select File dialog box.
3   In the dialog box, select the page to which you want to link.
4   Click Select to create the hyperlink.

Connecting Web pages **5–3**

```
┌─────────────────────────────────────────────────────────────┐
│                                                               │
│   [ About us || Locations || Products || Recipes || Feedback ] │
│                        🖑                                      │
│           © Outlander Spices 2001-2002. All rights reserved.  │
│                                                               │
└─────────────────────────────────────────────────────────────┘
```

Exhibit 5-1: A part of the Web page showing hyperlinks

Do it!

A-1: Creating a link to another Web page

Here's how	Here's why
1 Open Our_plans.htm	(In the Unit5 folder.) You'll create a link from this page to another page.
2 Select **Products**	Locations || **Products** || Recipes
	(Scroll down the document to find the text.) You'll make this text a hyperlink.
3 Choose **Modify, Make Link**	To open the Select File dialog box. A list of Web pages appears in the dialog box.
Select **Products.htm**	(In the Unit5 folder.) You'll create a link to this page.
Click **Select**	
4 Deselect and observe the text	Products
	The text is underlined and is a hyperlink.
5 Open the HTML Source inspector	
Observe the HTML code in the HTML Source inspector	`<a href="Products.htm">Products</a>`
	The A tag is used to create a hyperlink. The text enclosed within the A tag appears as a hyperlink. The HREF attribute of the A tag is used to specify the page to which the hyperlink links. Here, the text Products is linked to Products.htm.
Close the HTML Source inspector	

5–4 Dreamweaver 3.0: Basic

6 Update the document	
Preview in browser	You'll test the link.
7 Point as shown	Products
	The pointer changes to a hand indicating that it is a hyperlink.
8 Click the **Products** link	The Products page appears.
9 Click **Back**	(On the Standard toolbar of the Web browser.) To view the Our_plans page.
10 Click **Forward**	To view the Products page.
11 View the Our_plans page	Click Back.
Close the Web browser	

The drag and drop method

Explanation

Another way to create a text link is by using the drag and drop method. Just as the name implies, this method involves dragging a file to create the link, and this is how you do it:

1 Open the Site window, Document window, and Property inspector.

2 In the Document window, select the text that will be the link.

3 In the Site window, select the file that you want to create a link to and then drag it to the Link box of the Property inspector (as shown in Exhibit 5-2).

Connecting Web pages **5–5**

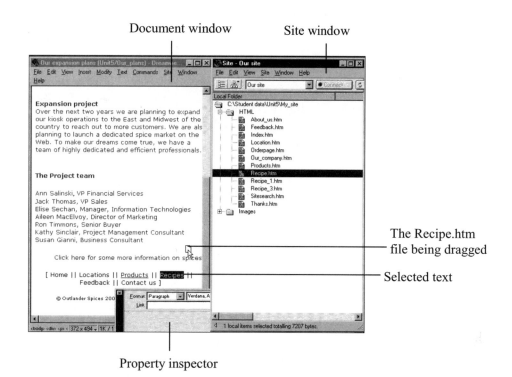

Exhibit 5-2: The drag and drop method to create a link

Do it! ## A-2: Creating a link by using the drag and drop method

Here's how	Here's why
1 Create a new local site	Choose Site, New Site.
Specify the name of the site as **Our site**	In the Site Name box of the Site Definition dialog box.
Select My_site as the root folder	(In the Unit5 folder.) Click the folder icon next to Local Root Folder box, select My_site, click Open and then click Select.
2 Click **OK**	
Click **Create**	To create a cache file for the site.
3 Hide the left pane of the Site window	If necessary.
4 Resize the Document window so that it and the Site window are visible	You'll create a hyperlink by using the drag and drop method.
5 In the Document window, select **Recipes**	Scroll down the document, if necessary.

6	In the Site window, expand the HTML folder	To view files in this folder.
	Select **Recipe.htm**	(Scroll down the Site window, if necessary.) You'll create a link to this page.
7	Drag Recipe.htm from the Site window to the Link box in the Property inspector as shown	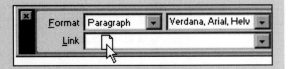
		(To create a hyperlink.) The path of the page appears in the Link box.
8	Deselect the text	
	Observe the HTML code in the HTML Source inspector	`<a href="My_site/HTML/Recipe.htm">Recipes</a>`
		It shows the A tag for the hyperlink to the Recipe page.
	Close the HTML Source inspector	
9	Update and preview the document in the Web browser	You'll test the hyperlink in the Web browser.
	Test the link	Click the Recipes link.
	Close the Web browser	
10	Close the Site window	
	Close the document	Do not close Dreamweaver.

Explanation

URLs

If you wanted to access Microsoft's Web site, you would have to specify its address in the address bar of the Web browser. A site's address is called the *URL*, or Uniform Resource Locator, and every Web site and page has one. Typically, URLs are composed of words, but you will also find numerical addresses, such as http://151.196.75.225/ being used to access a site.

Exhibit 5-3: The address bar of Internet Explorer showing the URL

A URL consists of three major components: protocol, host name and domain, and directory path. These components are separated by a forward slash (/). For example, the URL for a Microsoft page is shown in Exhibit 5-3.

The address bar shows http://www.microsoft.com/backstage/ where

- http:// is the protocol used.
- www.microsoft.com/ is the host name and domain of the server.
- backstage/ is the directory path where the page is stored. The path might also include file names.

Absolute and relative paths

You can specify the file path between the document you're linking to and from while creating links as either absolute or relative.

- *Absolute paths* include the complete path of the linked document and the protocol to use. These are generally used to link to a document that is not present in your Web site. For instance, http://www.microsoft/ie/default.htm is an absolute path. Absolute paths give the exact location of the document or file regardless of how the site is structured.

- *Relative paths* are used to link to a document that is part of your Web site and is present on your local system. You can specify the relative path from the document or from the root folder of the site. For instance, if you have a root folder, My site, storing the Index page and a subfolder called HTML storing the Products page, you can create a link from the Index page to the Products page by specifying the path as ../HTML/Products.htm. Here, the path is relative to the root folder. Relative paths are dependent upon the placement of pages and content in the directory structure of the site.

5–8 Dreamweaver 3.0: Basic

Do it!

A-3: Understanding absolute and relative paths

Here's how	Here's why
1 Open Links.htm	(In the Unit5 folder.) You'll identify paths in this document.
2 Select **here**	Scroll down the document.
Observe the Link box of the Property inspector	Link `://www.spiceguide.com/home/index.html` ▾
What path type is shown in the Link box?	
3 Select **Locations**	Located at the bottom of the page.
Observe the Link box of the Property inspector	Link `Location.htm`
What path type is shown in the Link box?	
4 Select **Recipes**	
Observe the Link box of the Property inspector	Link `HTML/Recipe.htm`
What path type is shown in the Link box?	*It is a relative path. It has the name of the subfolder, a forward slash, and the name of the document to which the link is created.*
5 Close the document	Do not close Dreamweaver.

Connecting Web pages **5–9**

Topic B: Creating links using named anchors

Explanation

Creating a text link from one page to another is merely one way you can use links. You can also make links within a single Web page, which is very useful for long documents. It helps visitors to jump quickly to another part of that same page without having to scroll. For example, you can have a list of recipe names at the top of the page, and users can click the recipe name to jump down the page and see the recipe details. For these links, you use *named anchors*. You can also use named anchors to create links to specific portions of other Web pages.

Named anchor

A named anchor is like a bookmark in a long document. You need to be careful in naming a named anchor because it is case sensitive. To create a named anchor:

1 Place the insertion point in the document where you want to create a named anchor.
2 Choose Insert, Named Anchor to open the Insert Named Anchor dialog box.
3 In the dialog box, enter the name of the named anchor.
4 Click OK to create the named anchor.

HTML code for named anchors

The HTML code that is generated when you create a named anchor is shown below:
```
<A NAME="GC"> </A>
```

The NAME attribute is used to name the point where the named anchor is created. In the HTML code given above, "GC" is the name of the named anchor. This name is used as the value for the HREF attribute when you create a link to this named anchor, as shown below.
```
<A HREF="#GC"> Green Cardamom </A>
```

In this HTML code, "Green Cardamom" is the text link pointing to the named anchor "GC," which is specified in the HREF attribute of the A tag. You need to prefix the name of the named anchor with the pound sign (#), which indicates that the link is to a named anchor.

5–10 Dreamweaver 3.0: Basic

Do it!

B-1: Creating a named anchor

Here's how	Here's why
1 Open Our_plans.htm	(In the Unit5 folder.) You'll create a named anchor in the document.
2 Place the insertion point as shown	**The Project team** Ann Salinski, VP Financial (Scroll down the document.). You'll create a named anchor for this subheading.
3 Choose **Insert**, **Named Anchor**	To open the Insert Named Anchor dialog box.
4 In the box, enter **Team**	*Insert Named Anchor* Anchor Name: `Team` OK Cancel Help
5 Click **OK**	
Observe the subheading	**The Project team** An anchor symbol appears before the subheading.
Observe the HTML code	`<a name="Team"></a>` (In the HTML Source inspector.)
Close the HTML Source inspector	
Observe the Property inspector	NamedAnchor Name `Team` The name of the named anchor appears in the Property inspector.
6 Create a named anchor **Expansion** for the subheading shown	**Expansion project** Over the next two years Choose Insert, Named Anchor and specify the name of the named anchor.
7 Update the document	

Links to named anchors

Explanation

After the named anchor is created, you need to create a link to it. To create this link, select the text that you want to link to the named anchor. In the Link box of the Property inspector, enter the name of the named anchor prefixed with the pound sign(#). This sign specifies that the link is to a named anchor. You can also link to a named anchor in another document. For example, you can create a link to a named anchor "Team" in the document "Project_plans.htm" by specifying the link as "Project_plans.htm#Team." Exhibit 5-4 shows a named anchor along with the text that is linked to it.

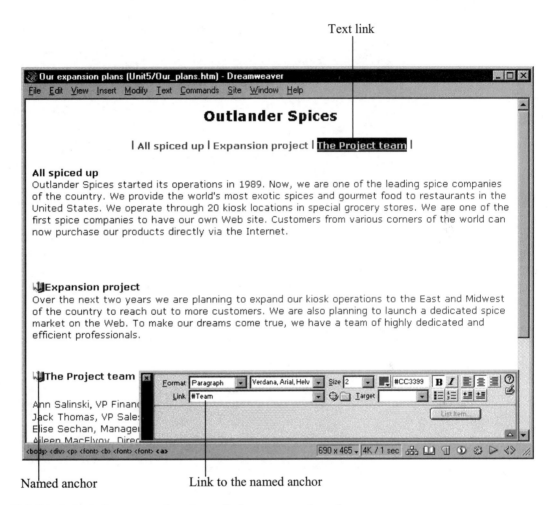

Exhibit 5-4: A document showing a link to a named anchor

5–12 Dreamweaver 3.0: Basic

Do it!

B-2: Linking to a named anchor

Here's how	Here's why
1 Select **The Project team**	Expansion project	**The Project team**	
	(The text is located at the top of the document.) You'll link this text to the named anchor before the subheading "The Project team."
2 In the Link box, enter **#Team**	In the Property inspector.
3 Deselect and observe the text	**The Project team**
	The text is underlined and the color of the text changes.
4 Update and preview the document in the Web browser	
5 Click the The Project team link	To go to the named anchor. You'll view the Project team members.
Click **Back**	
Close the Web browser	

The point-to-file icon

Explanation

You can easily create a link to a named anchor by using the point-to-file icon. Exhibit 5-6 shows the point-to-file icon pointing to a named anchor. To use this icon:

1. Select the text that you want to link to the named anchor.
2. In the Property inspector, click the point-to-file icon.
3. Drag the point-to-file icon to point to the named anchor.

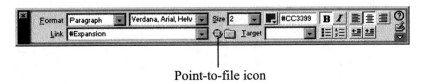

Point-to-file icon

Exhibit 5-5: The Property inspector with the point-to-file icon

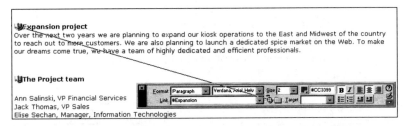

Exhibit 5-6: The point-to-file icon pointing to the Expansion named anchor

5–14 Dreamweaver 3.0: Basic

Do it! **B-3: Linking to a named anchor using the point-to-file icon**

Here's how	Here's why
1 Select **Expansion project**		Expansion project	The Project team	
	(In the beginning of the document.) You'll create a link to a named anchor.
2 Click the point-to-file icon	[Verdana, Arial, Helv ▾ Size 2 ▾ / ▾ 🖱 📁 Target]
	(In the Property inspector as shown in Exhibit 5-5.) You'll use this icon to point to the named anchor.
3 Drag the icon to point to the named anchor before the subheading Expansion project as in Exhibit 5-6	
Observe the Link box in the Property inspector	Link #Expansion ▾
	The name of the named anchor Expansion is prefixed with #.
Deselect the text	Expansion project
	The text is underlined and the text color changes.
4 Update and preview the document in the Web browser	
Test the link	Click the Expansion project link.
Close the Web browser	

Topic C: Linking to Web sites and e-mail addresses

Explanation

Links are a great way to offer variety to your users. For example, many Web sites will list links to other Web sites that have similar or more information. Another service many Web sites will include is an e-mail link. Visitors use this link to send feedback about your Web site.

Linking to Web sites

To create a link to another Web site, select the text on which you want to create the hyperlink, and in the Link box of the Property inspector, enter the URL of the Web site you want to link to, as shown in Exhibit 5-7.

Exhibit 5-7: The Link box with the Web site URL

Do it!

C-1: Linking to a Web site

Here's how	Here's why
1 Select **here** as shown	Click here for some more information on spices.
	(Scroll down, if necessary.) You'll link this text to a Web site.
2 In the Link box, enter http://www.msn.com	
Press ⏎ ENTER	
Deselect and observe the text	Click here for
3 Update and preview the document in the Web browser	The home page of the site appears.
Test the link	Click the here link.
Close the Web browser	

Linking to e-mail addresses

Explanation

A link that points to an e-mail address is known as a *mailto* link, and this is how it works. You use a mailto link to identify a particular e-mail address. When users click the link, the browser activates the default e-mail application and a blank message is displayed with the e-mail address you defined in the "To" field. The users fill in a subject and the body of the message and send you their order, feedback or query.

To create mailto links, select the text, and in the Link box of the Property inspector, enter the e-mail address of the recipient.

Exhibit 5-8: The Link box with the mailto link

Do it!

C-2: Linking to an e-mail address

Here's how	Here's why
1 Select **Contact Us**	Feedback || Contact us]
	You'll create a mailto link.
2 In the Link box, enter **mailto:contactus@outlanderspices.com**	(As shown in Exhibit 5-8.) To specify a mailto link.
Press (↵ ENTER)	
3 Update and preview document in the Web browser	You'll test the mailto link.
Click on the Contact us link	
If necessary, click Cancel	To close the Internet Connection Wizard.
4 Observe the screen	A new message window appears with the recipient's address.
5 Close the message window	(Choose File, Close.) Do not save changes.
Close the Web browser and the document	Do not close Dreamweaver.

Connecting Web pages **5–17**

Unit summary: Connecting Web pages

Topic A
In this unit, you learned how to **create links to other Web pages** and **use the drag and drop method** to create links. You also learned about **absolute** and **relative paths.**

Topic B
Next, you learned how to **create named anchors.** You also learned to **create a link to a named anchor** using the Property inspector and the **point-to-file icon.**

Topic C
Finally, you learned how to **create links to Web sites** and **e-mail addresses.**

Independent practice activity

1 Open Outlander_Spices.htm. (In the Unit5 folder.)

2 Create a link on the text Recipe of the day!! to the document Recipe_3.htm.

3 Update the document and test the link in the Web browser.

4 Close the Web browser.

5 Create a link on the text Outlander Spices to **www.outlanderspices@Outlander.com.** (You'll not be able to link to this site.)

6 At the end of the first paragraph, select the text suggestion and create a link to **getintouch@outlanderspices.com.**

7 Update the document.

8 Create a named anchor **Top** before the heading "Welcome to Outlander Spices."

9 At the bottom of the page, select the text Back to top and create a link to the named anchor **Top.**

10 Update the document and test the link in the Web browser.

11 Close the Web browser and the document.

5–18 Dreamweaver 3.0: Basic

Unit 6
Working with images

Unit time: 40 minutes

Complete this unit and you'll know how to:

A Insert an image, modify its alignment, and align the text around it.

B Add a background image to a Web page.

C Create links by using an image, image map, and text label for an image.

6–2 Dreamweaver 3.0: Basic

Topic A: Inserting an image in a document

Explanation

Images and graphics are effective ways of communicating with viewers of your Web site. They add an artistic touch to your Web page by enhancing its appearance. For example, you can add images to the Products page of Outlander Spices Web site to highlight spices. You can also align text around an image to improve its readability.

Images in a Web page

When you use images on a Web page, be sure to keep file size in mind. A large image takes more time to load. So, most Web designers will use images with a small file size to keep the overall page size as small as possible. Another common practice is to compress images to reduce size. Ideally, the size of the Web page should be around 30KB.

You have three main sources for your Web site images. First, you can find images free on the Web, meaning a Web site that denotes that its images can be freely used. Don't take images from other Web sites without permission because that would be a copyright infringement. Second, you can purchase a collection of images on CD-ROM or from a Web site that sells them. Third, you can create the images yourself. Obviously, Dreamweaver is not the application with which to create Web images, but other Macromedia products, such as Fireworks, provide easy ways to create your own graphics.

There are many formats for graphic files, but two are used most often – Graphic Interchange File (GIF) and Joint Photographic Experts Group (JPEG). The GIF format is used for line drawings, such as bar charts, and images with a few solid colors. The JPEG format is used for photographic images and other images that use numerous colors and shades of colors, making JPEG more useful for some purposes than GIF. On the other hand, a GIF file will allow you to define one color as transparent, which is very useful. The size of a GIF is smaller than a JPEG and therefore downloads faster than a JPEG.

You can add an image to a document by placing the insertion point where you want to insert the image and choose Insert, Image. In the Select Image Source dialog box, select the image of your choice. Click Select to insert the image.

Working with images   **6–3**

The IMG tag

When you insert an image on a Web page, the IMG tag is added in the HTML code. It is a container tag and its attributes are described in the following table:

Attribute	Description
SRC	Specifies the URL or location of the image file.
ALIGN	Specifies the alignment of the text around the image.
BORDER	Specifies the size of the border around the image.
HEIGHT	Specifies the height of the image. It also helps in resizing the image.
WIDTH	Specifies the width of the image. It also helps in resizing the image. Setting this along with the HEIGHT attribute creates a placeholder for the image that helps in faster downloading of the Web page containing the image. This is because the browser doesn't have to figure out the size of the image.
HSPACE	Specifies the horizontal margin to be placed around the image.
VSPACE	Specifies the vertical margin to be placed around the image.
ALT	Specifies alternative text if the browser does not support images or if images are turned off.

Do it!

A-1: Inserting an image

Here's how	Here's why
1 Open Spicy_recipe.htm	(In the Unit6 folder.) You'll insert an image in this document.
Verify that the insertion point is at the top of the page	Chicken stuffed with spices You'll insert an image here.
2 Choose **Insert**, **Image**	To open the Select Image Source dialog box.
3 Select **recipe3.gif**	(In the Unit6 folder.) You'll insert this image in the document. A preview of the image appears in the Image Preview pane of the dialog box.
4 Click **Select**	To close the Select Image Source dialog box and insert the image.
Observe the HTML code	`<img src="recipe3.gif" width="132" height="127">` (In the HTML Source inspector.) The IMG tag is used to add an image in a document. The SRC attribute specifies the path and the file name of the image file.

> 5 Close the HTML Source inspector
>
>   Update the document

Image properties

Explanation

You can modify a number of properties of an image: width, height, border, and alignment. Aligning an image to the left, right, or center and adjusting its height and width can enhance the appearance of a Web page. You can use the Property inspector to modify image properties (as shown in Exhibit 6-1).

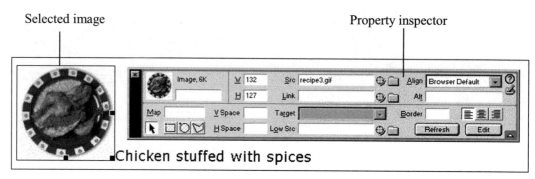

Exhibit 6-1: The Property inspector and the selected image

The properties of the Property inspector are described in the following table:

Property	Description
W	Specifies the width of the image.
H	Specifies the height of the image.
Src	Specifies the location or URL of the source file for the image.
Link	Specifies the path of the file to which the image is linked.
Align	Specifies the alignment of the text around the image, relative to the image.
Alt	Specifies the alternative text for the image if the browser does not support images or if images are turned off.
Border	Specifies the border width, in pixels, around the image.
V Space	Specifies the vertical spacing, in pixels, for the image.
H Space	Specifies the horizontal spacing, in pixels, for the image.
Low Src	Specifies the image that should load before the main image. Most Web designers use a black and white version of the main image because it loads faster and gives viewers an idea of what the main image displays.

You'll use some of these properties later in the unit.

To align an image, select the image and choose Text, Alignment, and the alignment of your choice or use the Property inspector.

Do it!

A-2: Modifying the alignment and size of an image

Here's how	Here's why
1 Select and observe the image	(If necessary.) The image is aligned to the left of the page. You'll align it to the center.
2 Click [icon]	(Expand the Property inspector.) To center align the image.
3 In the W box, enter **135**	(In the Property inspector.) To resize the image by setting its width.
4 In the H box, enter **130**	(In the Property inspector.) To resize the image by setting its height.
Press TAB	Note that the image is center aligned and the size of the image increases.
5 Observe the HTML code	```<p align="center"><font size="4" face="Verdana, Arial, Helvetica, sans-serif" color="#660066"> <img src="recipe3.gif" width="135" height="130"> Chicken stuffed with spices</font></p>```
	(In the HTML Source inspector.) The ALIGN attribute of the P tag is used to align the image.
Close the HTML Source inspector	
6 Update the document	

Formatting text around an image

Explanation By default, when you insert an image in a Web page, the text around it aligns to the bottom of the image, as shown in Exhibit 6-2. You can format the text around the image if you desire. Exhibit 6-3 shows an image with text aligned at the top.

Exhibit 6-2: An image with text aligned at the bottom

Exhibit 6-3: An image with the text aligned at the top

You can also add horizontal and vertical spacing between the image and text to organize the Web page proportionally. You can use the Align list of the Property inspector to do so. The following table explains the alignment options available in the Align list of the Property inspector:

Alignment	Description
Browser default	The default alignment that the browser supports; it varies from browser to browser.
Baseline	Aligns the baseline of the text to the bottom of the selected image.
Absolute bottom	Aligns the absolute bottom of the text with the bottom of the selected image.
Bottom	Aligns the baseline of the text to the bottom of the selected image.
Top	Aligns the top of the tallest character in the text with the top of the selected image.
Text top	Aligns the tallest character in the text with the top of the selected image.
Middle	Aligns the baseline of the text with the middle of the selected image.
Absolute middle	Aligns the middle of the text with the middle of the selected image.
Left	Aligns the selected image to the left and wraps the text around it to the right.
Right	Aligns the selected image to the right and wraps the text around it to the left.

Do it! ## A-3: Aligning text around an image

Here's how	Here's why
1 Select the image	![Chicken stuffed with spices]
	(If necessary.) The text is aligned to the bottom of the image. You'll align the text around the image.
2 From the Align list, select **Absolute Middle**	(In the Property inspector.) To align the text centrally around the image.
3 Click the expander arrow	(If necessary.) To view more properties of the selected image.
In the H Space box, enter **20**	H Space 20
	To provide a space of 20 pixels between the text and the image.
Press (TAB)	The space between the image and the text increases.
4 Observe the HTML code	```<img src="recipe3.gif" width="135" height="130" align="absmiddle" hspace="20">```
	The ALIGN attribute of the IMG tag specifies the alignment of the text around the image. The HSPACE attribute specifies the horizontal spacing between the image and the text.
Close the HTML Source inspector	
5 Update the document	

Topic B: Adding background images

Explanation

Sometimes you'll come across Web pages with colored backgrounds, but some use a background image instead. Background images provide a distinctive look to a Web site, making it easily identifiable to users.

Background images

A Web page can be very long and to set a background image for it means to have an equally long image. Most Web designers prefer using a smaller background image. When a small image is set as a background for the Web page, it repeats on the page until it fills the entire page with its copies. This is known as *tiling*.

When you insert a background image, make sure it does not affect the readability of the page. A good Web practice is to use images with pastels or washed-out colors. Generally, *textures* are used as backgrounds in Web pages. Texture is the roughness or the feel of a surface.

To add a background image:

1. Open the document in which you want to add a background image.
2. Choose Modify, Page Properties to open the Page Properties dialog box.
3. In the dialog box, click Browse to locate the image file that you want to set as the background image.
4. Click Select to select the image.
5. Click OK.

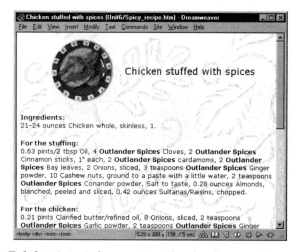

Exhibit 6-4: A document with a background image

Do it!

B-1: Adding a background image

Here's how	Here's why
1 Choose **Modify, Page Properties...**	
2 Click **Browse**	(This button is next to the Background Image box.) To open the Select Image Source dialog box to locate the background image.
Select **Background.gif**	(In the Unit6 folder.) A preview of the image appears in the Image Preview pane of the dialog box.
3 Click **Select**	Background Image: Background.gif
	The name of the image file appears in the Background Image box.
4 Click **OK**	A background image is added to the document, as shown in Exhibit 6-4.
5 Observe the HTML code	```<body bgcolor="#FFFFFF" background="Background.gif">```
	The BACKGROUND attribute of the BODY tag specifies the background image of the document.
Close the HTML Source inspector	
6 Update and preview the document in the Web browser	The Web page has a background image.
Close the Web browser and the document	Do not close Dreamweaver.

6–10 Dreamweaver 3.0: Basic

Topic C: Creating links by using images

Explanation

If you were to design a Web site with only text, your site would be pretty boring. The same can be said for the links on your site. Text links are useful, but lack the visual appeal you get when you use an image as a link. For example, if you wanted a site to link to all Outlander Spices' store locations in the United States, you wouldn't want to list link after link when you could use an image of a US map with links defined at the appropriate places. There is no comparison: the map is much more dynamic and would add to the overall appeal of the site.

Page links with images

You can use images not only to enhance the appearance of a page, but also to create hyperlinks. After you create links on an image, you should ensure that the links work properly by testing them in a Web browser.

To link an image to a page:

1 Select the image and choose Modify, Make Link to open the Select File dialog box.

2 In the dialog box, select the page to which you want to link your image.

3 Click Select to close the dialog box.

You can also use the Property inspector to create a link by specifying the page name in the Link box.

Do it!

C-1: Creating a link by using an image

Here's how	Here's why
1 Open Our_outlets.htm	In the Unit6 folder.
Select the image as shown	
	(Scroll down the document.) You'll create a link using this image.
2 Choose **Modify, Make Link**	The Select File dialog box appears.
Select **Products.htm**	(In the Unit6 folder.) You'll create a link to the Products page.
Click **Select**	

Working with images   6-11

3 Observe the HTML code

```
<a href="Products.htm">
  <img src="cloves.gif"
  width="87" height="87"
  hspace="5" border="0"
  align="absmiddle"></a>
```

The A tag is used to link an image to another Web page.

Close the HTML Source inspector

Update and preview the document in the Web browser

4 Point to the linked image

The pointer changes to a hand indicating that the image is a hyperlink.

Click the image   To view the Products page.

5 Navigate back to Our_outlets page

Close the Web browser

Image maps

Explanation

Surfing the Web, you may come across images that contain many links instead of a single link. Such images are called *image maps*. You can create links from different areas of the same image to different pages or sections of a Web page. The difference between an image link and an image map is that an image link can have only a single link and an image map can have as many links as you can put in it.

Hotspots

Each distinct area in an image map that is defined as a hyperlink is called a *hotspot*. Clicking the hotspot takes you to the respective link. For instance, on an image map, you can show the locations of your company's branches, and link each location to a separate page (or part of the same page). You need to create named anchors in the document before creating an image map to link to a section of the same document.

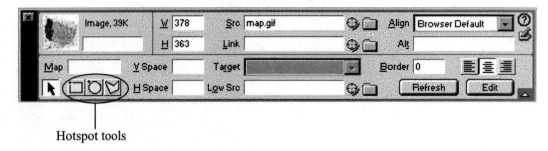

Hotspot tools

Exhibit 6-5: The Property inspector with Hotspot tools

There are three tools available in Dreamweaver to create hotspots, as shown in Exhibit 6-5. These are the Rectangular Hotspot Tool, Oval Hotspot Tool, and Polygon Hotspot Tool and are used to create hotspots of their respective shapes. For example, for an irregular area, you can use the Polygon Hotspot Tool and for a circular area, you can use the Oval Hotspot Tool. After creating a hotspot on the image map, you need to link it to another Web page or a named anchor.

You can move, edit, and delete a hotspot. Moving a hotspot is easy. You just need to select it and drag it to the new location. You can edit the hotspot by resizing it, as shown in Exhibit 6-6. For deleting a hotspot, select the hotspot and press the Delete key.

Exhibit 6-6: A hotspot being resized

To create an image map:
1 Select the image.
2 Click the expander arrow on the Property inspector to view the Hotspot tools.
3 Select the Hotspot tool of your choice (as shown in Exhibit 6-5).
4 Define the image map area by dragging the pointer over the image to create a hotspot.
5 In the Link box of the Property inspector, specify the name of the page or the named anchor to which you want to create a link.

Working with images   **6–13**

Do it!   **C-2: Creating an image map**

Here's how	Here's why
1 Select the image of the map	Scroll up.
2 On the Property inspector, click	(The Rectangular Hotspot Tool is in the Property inspector.) Note that the pointer changes to a cross when you place it over the selected image.
3 Point to Oregon in the image	You'll insert a hotspot for this state.
Drag in the state to draw a rectangle as shown	
	This is the hotspot for Oregon. You'll create a link from this hotspot.
4 In the Link box, enter **Oregon**	Link #Oregon
	To specify the name of the named anchor. You'll create a link from the rectangular hotspot to this named anchor.
Observe the HTML code	```<area shape="rect" coords="45,100,92,131" href="#Oregon"></map>```
	The AREA tag creates a clickable area in an image to link to the Web page or named anchor. The COORDS attribute specifies the pixel coordinates of the area.
Close the HTML Source inspector	
5 Click	(In the Property inspector.) You'll create a polygon hotspot.
6 Point to Nevada on the map	The pointer takes the shape of a cross. When you click, you'll define the first corner of the polygon.
Click at the indicated position	

	Click at the indicated position	
		To create the first edge of the polygon.
	Click at the indicated position	
		To create the second and third edge of the polygon.
	Click at the indicated position	
		To create the fourth edge of the polygon.
	Click at the indicated position	
		To complete the polygon.
7	Link this hotspot to the **Nevada** named anchor	In the Link box of the Property inspector, enter Nevada.
8	Update and preview the document in the Web browser	
9	Point to Oregon as shown	
		The pointer changes to a hand indicating that it is a hyperlink.
	Click **Oregon**	To go to the linked part of the document. A listing of Outlander Spices' outlets in Oregon appears on the Web page.
10	Click **Back**	To go to the top of the Web page.
11	Test the Nevada hotspot link	Point to Nevada and click.
	Close the Web browser	

Working with images   **6–15**

Alternatives for images

Explanation   Sometimes, viewers will customize their browser so that images are not displayed, helping pages to load quickly. With that in mind, it is a good practice to specify alternative text for those viewers or those that use text-only Web browsers. The alternative text gives users some information about the image such as a caption or brief description, and will appear instead of the image on the page.

Even when the image does appear on the page, you can view the text by pointing to the image and leaving the mouse pointer there for a moment. This is known as the *text label*.

To create a text label for an image, select the image. In the Alt box of the Property inspector, specify the text you want to display.

Do it!   ### C-3: Creating a text label for an image

Here's how	Here's why
1 Select the image named map.gif	You'll insert a text label for this image
2 In the Alt box, enter **Outlander Spices Outlets**	(In the Property inspector.) This is the text label for the image.
3 Observe the HTML code	```<img src="map.gif" width="378" height="363" border="0" usemap="#Map" alt="Outlander Spices Outlets">```
	The ALT attribute of the IMG tag specifies the text label for the image.
Close the HTML Source inspector	
4 Update and preview the document in the Web browser	
5 Point to the map image	You'll view the text label you specified.
Observe the image	
	The text label for the image appears.
6 Close the Web browser and the document	Do not close Dreamweaver.

6-16 Dreamweaver 3.0: Basic

Unit summary: Working with images

Topic A In this unit, you learned how to **insert an image** in a document, **modify the alignment of an image**, and **align text around an image**.

Topic B Next, you learned how to **add a background image** to a document.

Topic C Finally, you learned how to **create links using an image, an image map**, and a **text label for an image**.

Independent practice activity

1 Open Products_info.htm. Insert cinnamon.gif before the subheading Cinnamon. (Both files are in the Unit6 folder.)

2 Insert nutmeg.gif before the subheading Nutmeg and cloves.gif before the subheading Cloves. (The images are in the Unit6 folder.)

3 Center align the spice images and the subheadings next to them.

4 Insert Back.gif as the background image of the document.

5 Select the Recipes image at the end of the document and link it to Recipe.htm.

6 Update the document and test the link in the Web browser.

7 Close the Web browser and the document.

8 Open Recipe_list.htm. (In the Unit6 folder.)

9 Create oval hotspots on both the recipe images. (Hint: Select the Oval Hotspot Tool from the Property inspector and create hotspots.)

10 Link the hotspot on the first recipe image to Recipe_1.htm. Link the hotspot on the second recipe image to Recipe_3.htm. (Hint: In the Link box, enter the file name without # and with the file extension.)

11 Create two text labels, **Princely Potatoes** for the first recipe image and **Chicken stuffed with spices** for the second recipe image.

12 Update the document.

13 Test the link and the text label in the Web browser.

14 Close the Web browser and the document.

Unit 7
Creating tables

Unit time: 70 minutes

Complete this unit and you'll know how to:

A Add a table, add text to it, add and delete rows and columns, import tabular data in a Dreamweaver document, and insert images in a table.

B Select tables, rows, and columns, format tables headings, align text, and modify table properties.

C Change the width, cell spacing, and cell padding of a table, merge cells, and remove table borders.

D Design a Web page by using nested tables and invisible graphics.

Topic A: Adding tables

Explanation

Tables in Dreamweaver are no different from tables that you find in books or any other documents. A table can be an effective way of presenting complex information, such as a product list or a reference table. You can also use tables as a design tool because they make it easier to combine and align text, pictures, and white space. Most of the common Web sites you see on the Internet are designed by using tables.

Tables

A table is composed of rows and columns with data in individual *cells*. A cell is an intersection of a row and column.

To insert a table:

1. Place the insertion point where you want to insert the table.
2. Choose Insert, Table to open the Insert Table dialog box.
3. Specify the number of rows and columns in the table.
4. Click OK.

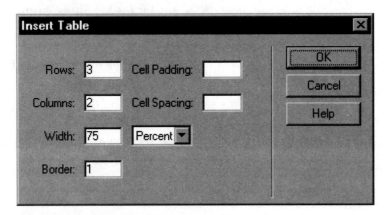

Exhibit 7-1: The Insert Table dialog box

TABLE tags

When you add a table in a document, the HTML code generates the TABLE tags. It is a container tag and is the primary tag that surrounds the rest of the text and the code within the table. The TR tag defines each row in a table and the TD tag defines the data of each cell.

Creating tables   **7–3**

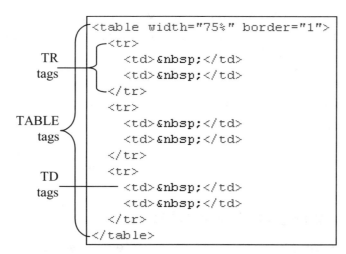

Exhibit 7-2: The HTML code for tables

In the HTML code shown in Exhibit 7-2, the TABLE tags surround the rest of the text and the code within the table. Three TR tags within the TABLE tags indicate there are three rows in the table. Two TD tags within each pair of the TR tags indicate there are two columns. Each pair of the TD tags encloses the data in the respective cell. At this time, all the cells are empty.

Do it!

A-1: Inserting a table

Here's how	Here's why
1 In the Document window, verify that a blank document is open	You'll insert a table in a blank document.
2 Choose **Insert**, **Table**	To open the Insert Table dialog box.
3 Verify that 3 is selected in the Rows box	To specify the numbers of rows in the table.
4 In the Columns box, enter **2**	(As shown in Exhibit 7-1.) To specify the number of columns in the table.
5 Click **OK**	(To insert a table.) A table with three rows and two columns appears in the blank document.
Observe the HTML code	(As shown in Exhibit 7-2.) The TABLE tags are the primary tags that surround the rest of the text and the code within the table. The TR tags define each row in a table and the TD tags define the data of each cell.
Close the HTML Source inspector	

7–4 Dreamweaver 3.0: Basic

Adding text

Explanation

A table is not meaningful without data. You can add text, images, links, and other objects in a table. To add text to the table, place the insertion point in the cell where you want to enter text and type the text.

Cinnamon	$10.75
Nutmeg	$3.95
Bay leaf	$5.75

Exhibit 7-3: A table with three rows and two columns

Do it!

A-2: Adding text in a table

Here's how	Here's why
1 Place the insertion point in the first cell	You'll add text in this cell.
2 Type **Cinnamon**	To specify the text for the first cell.
3 Press (TAB)	To move the insertion point to the next cell.
4 Enter text in the other cells as shown in Exhibit 7-3	
Observe the HTML code	

```
<table width="75%" border="1">
   <tr>
      <td>Cinnamon</td>
      <td>$10.75</td>
   </tr>
   <tr>
      <td>Nutmeg</td>
      <td>$3.95</td>
   </tr>
   <tr>
      <td>Bay leaf</td>
      <td>$5.75</td>
   </tr>
</table>
```

The TR tags define each row in a table and the TD tags define each cell's data. The two TD tags between each TR tag indicate that the table has two columns.

Close the HTML Source inspector

Creating tables **7–5**

Inserting rows and columns

Explanation

Once a table exists on the page, you can expand it by adding rows and columns. For example, let's say you have a table with two columns and three rows containing names and prices. You could add a row at the top for a descriptive heading and insert an additional column for product code information, like the table shown in Exhibit 7-4.

To insert rows and columns:

1 Place the insertion point in the cell where you want to insert a row or column.
2 Choose Modify, Table, Insert Rows or Columns to open the Insert Rows or Columns dialog box.
3 Select whether you want to insert rows or columns, specify the number to be inserted, and select whether it should be inserted before or after the current row or column.

When you are in the last cell of a table, pressing Tab will automatically add a new row. This is very useful when you're not sure how many rows you'll need.

Product code	Product name	Price/12 oz.
CM01	Cinnamon	$10.75
NM01	Nutmeg	$3.95
BL01	Bay leaf	$5.75

Exhibit 7-4: An additional row and column inserted in the table

Do it!

A-3: Inserting a row and a column

Here's how	Here's why
1 Place the insertion point in the first cell of the table	You'll insert a row at the beginning of the table.
2 Choose **Modify, Table, Insert Rows or Columns...**	To open the Insert Rows or Columns dialog box.
Select as shown	Insert: ⦿ Rows ○ Columns Number of Rows: 1 Where: ⦿ Above the Selection ○ Below the Selection
Click **OK**	A row is inserted at the beginning of the table.

3 Choose **Modify**, **Table**, **Insert Rows or Columns...**	You'll insert a column in the table.
Select as shown	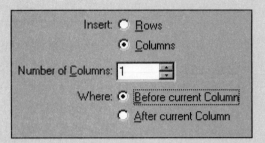
Click **OK**	A column is added at the beginning of the table. The table now has four rows and three columns.
4 Enter text in the cells as shown in Exhibit 7-4	
Observe the HTML code between the TABLE tags	```<table width="75%" border="1">
<tr>
<td>Product code</td>
<td>Product name</td>
<td>Price/12 oz.</td>
</tr>```
	The code now has four TR tags, one for each row. The three TD tags between each TR tag indicate that the table has three columns.
Close the HTML Source inspector	
5 Place insertion point in the last cell as shown	$5.75
Press TAB	To add a new row.

Creating tables   **7-7**

Deleting rows and columns

Explanation   You can delete rows or columns that you no longer need. To delete them, place the insertion point in the row or column that you want to delete. Choose Modify, Table, Delete Column to delete a column and Delete Row to delete a row.

Do it!   ## A-4: Deleting a row

Here's how	Here's why
1 Place the insertion point in the last row of the table	If necessary.
2 Choose **Modify**, **Table**, **Delete Row**	(To delete this row.) The table now has four rows.
3 Save the document as **Productdata.htm**	In the Unit7 folder.
Observe the HTML code	The code has four TR tags, one for each row.
Close the HTML Source inspector	
Close the document	Do not close Dreamweaver.

Importing tabular data

Explanation   Suppose you have some tabular data in an application and you want to put it on a Web page. To do this, you can import tabular data into Dreamweaver from other applications such as Notepad or Microsoft Excel. You can only import data if the original data is saved in a *delimited format*. In a delimited format, tabs, commas, or other delimiters separate the data.

To import tabular data:
1   Place the insertion point where you want to import table data.
2   Choose File, Import, Import Table Data to open the Import Table Data dialog box.
3   Click Browse to locate the file containing tabular data.
4   Select the file.
5   From the Delimiter list, select the delimiter.
6   Click OK.

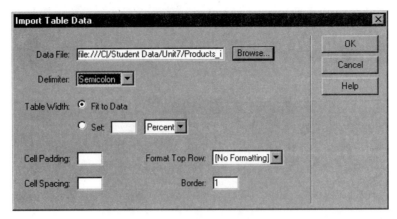

Exhibit 7-5: The Import Table Data dialog box

Do it!

A-5: Inserting tabular data

Here's how	Here's why
1 Open Products_info.txt	(Open the file in Notepad.) To view the contents of the text file.
Observe the contents of this file	The contents are in normal text format and not in table format. The data are separated by semicolon (;). You'll import these data into a Dreamweaver document.
Close Notepad	
2 Activate the Document window	If necessary.
Choose **File**, **Import**, **Import Table Data...**	To open the Import Table Data dialog box.
3 Click **Browse**	
Select **Products_info.txt**	(In the Unit7 folder.) This is a text file that has tabular data.
Click **Open**	The path of the file appears in the Data File box.
4 From the Delimiter list, select **Semicolon**	To specify the delimiter in the text file.
5 Under Table Width, verify that Fit to Data is selected	(As shown in Exhibit 7-5.) You'll create a table that adjusts to the longest text string in each column.

Creating tables　**7–9**

6 Click **OK**	The data from the text file is imported into a table.
7 Save the document as **Spices.htm**	
Observe the HTML code	The code for the table is between the <TABLE> and </TABLE> tags.
Close the HTML Source inspector	

Images in a table

Explanation

You insert images in table cells in the same way as you would anywhere else on a Web page. This is a benefit because it gives you greater control over where the image will appear on the page. For example, let's say you insert an image into a cell and then change the alignment from left to right. The alignment change is relative to the cell instead of across the entire browser window.

Once you insert an image in a cell, you vertically align it to the top, middle, bottom, baseline, or to the browser's default (usually middle) by using the Vert property of the cell in the Property inspector. You can also align the image horizontally by using the Horz property of the cell.

To add an image to a table, place the insertion point in the cell in which you want to add the image and choose Insert, Image to open the Select Image Source dialog box. You then select the image and click Select.

Product Name	Product Description	Price
Cinnamon	A common ingredient in apple pies, it is also used to treat nausea, vomiting, diarrhea, and indigestion.	$10.75
Nutmeg	The aroma of nutmeg livens up vegetables, sauces, cheese dishes, and soups. It is a sure cure for digestive disorders.	$3.95
Cloves	They can be tasted studded in baked ham, breads, and cakes and in mulled wine. It is used to relieve dental aches and check the symptoms of cholera and asthma.	$8.75

Exhibit 7-6: A table with images

7–10 Dreamweaver 3.0: Basic

Do it!

A-6: Inserting an image in a table

Here's how	Here's why
1 Place the insertion point before **Cinnamon**	You'll insert an image in this cell.
2 Choose **Insert**, **Image**	To open the Select Image Source dialog box.
3 Select **cinnamon.gif**	(In the Unit7 folder.) You'll insert this image.
4 Click **Select**	The image is inserted in the cell.
5 Insert nutmeg.gif before Nutmeg and cloves.gif before Cloves, as shown in Exhibit 7-6	
6 Update the document	

Topic B: Formatting tables

Explanation

When it comes to formatting a table, you have two options—formatting the text within a table and formatting the table itself. Text is formatted just as you would any other text in a Dreamweaver document, and a table is formatted by changing the table properties.

Selecting a table

You need to select the table to format it. To select a table, position the insertion point to the top left corner of the table and click when the four headed arrow appears. You can also choose Modify, Table, Select Table to select the table. Handles appear around the table when it is selected.

Selecting rows or columns

To select a row, position the insertion point to the left margin of the row and click when the selection arrow appears. Similarly, you can select a column by positioning the insertion point to the top of the column and clicking.

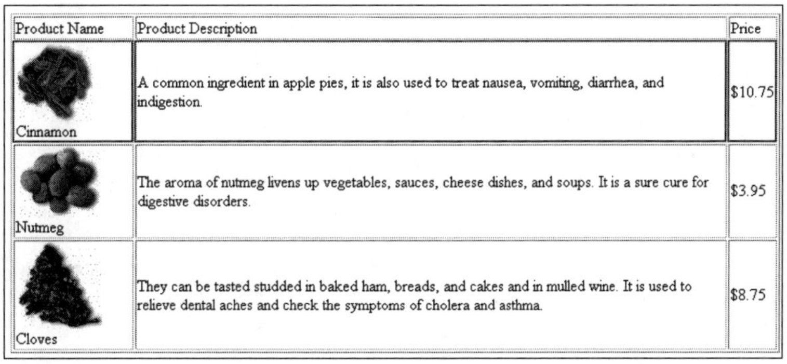

Product Name	Product Description	Price
Cinnamon	A common ingredient in apple pies, it is also used to treat nausea, vomiting, diarrhea, and indigestion.	$10.75
Nutmeg	The aroma of nutmeg livens up vegetables, sauces, cheese dishes, and soups. It is a sure cure for digestive disorders.	$3.95
Cloves	They can be tasted studded in baked ham, breads, and cakes and in mulled wine. It is used to relieve dental aches and check the symptoms of cholera and asthma.	$8.75

Exhibit 7-7: A selected row in a table

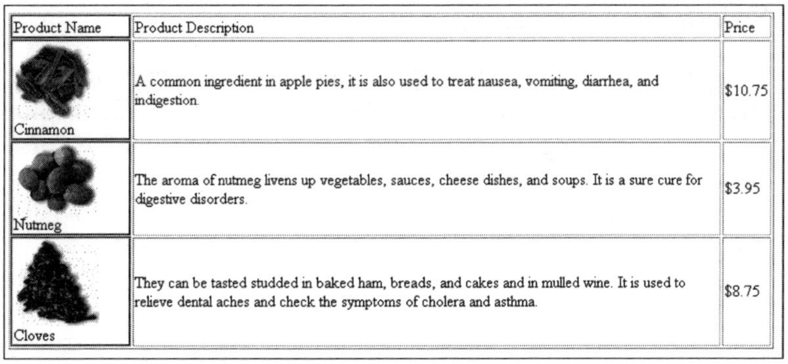

Product Name	Product Description	Price
Cinnamon	A common ingredient in apple pies, it is also used to treat nausea, vomiting, diarrhea, and indigestion.	$10.75
Nutmeg	The aroma of nutmeg livens up vegetables, sauces, cheese dishes, and soups. It is a sure cure for digestive disorders.	$3.95
Cloves	They can be tasted studded in baked ham, breads, and cakes and in mulled wine. It is used to relieve dental aches and check the symptoms of cholera and asthma.	$8.75

Exhibit 7-8: A selected column in a table

7–12 Dreamweaver 3.0: Basic

Do it!

B-1: Selecting a table, row, and column

Here's how	Here's why
1 Position the insertion point to the top left corner of the table	*(four-headed arrow over a table cell labeled "Product Name")*
	A four-headed arrow appears.
Click the selection arrow	To select the table.
Deselect the table	Click outside the table.
2 Position the insertion point to the left margin of the second row	*(selection arrow pointing at a row)*
	The selection arrow appears.
Click the selection arrow	To select the second row as shown in Exhibit 7-7.
Deselect the row	
3 Position the insertion point to the top margin of the first column	*(downward arrow over a column labeled "Product Name")*
	The selection arrow appears.
Click the selection arrow	To select the first column as shown in Exhibit 7-8.
Deselect the column	

Table headings

Explanation

A common format applied to text within a table is table headings. Table headings provide information about the table's data and are easily distinguished from other rows. To create a heading in a table, select the row and from the Format list in the Property inspector, select the heading style of your choice.

Creating tables **7–13**

Do it!

B-2: Formatting table headings

Here's how	Here's why
1 Select the table	If necessary.
2 Set the font to Verdana, Arial, Helvetica, sans-serif and the font size to 2	
3 Select the first row	
From the Format list, select **Heading 1**	(The Format list is in the Property inspector.) To apply the Heading 1 format to the entire row.
4 Update the document	

Text alignment

Explanation

You can change the alignment of text in a table to the left, right, or center, which will modify the appearance but not the position of the table. To align text, select the row or column that you want to align, and then in the Property inspector, click on the appropriate alignment button.

Do it!

B-3: Aligning text

Here's how	Here's why
1 Select the first row	(If necessary.) You'll align the text of this row.
2 Click	(In the Property inspector.) The text in the first row is aligned to the center.
3 Update the document	

Table properties

Explanation

You can give a distinct look to a table by setting its properties. There are some properties you set for a table as a whole, including border style, background color, background image, and border color. Exhibit 7-9 displays the Property inspector with the various table properties.

Each cell, row, and column also has its own properties that can be changed such as background color, border color, and background image.

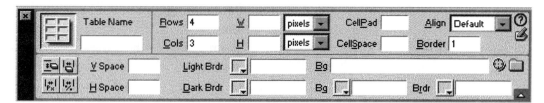

Exhibit 7-9: The Property inspector with table properties

Modifying table properties

The following table lists the various table properties that you can modify:

Property	Description
Table Name	Specifies the table name.
Rows	Specifies the number of rows in the table.
Columns	Specifies the number of columns in the table.
W	Specifies the width of the table and can be specified in pixels or percentage of the browser window.
H	Specifies the height of the table and can be specified in pixels or percentage of the browser window.
CellPad	Specifies the spacing, in pixels, between the cell content and the gridlines of the table.
CellSpace	Specifies the thickness, in pixels, of the gridlines of the table.
Align	Specifies the alignment of the table relative to other content on the page. This can be specified as Left, Right, Center, or Default. Default is the default alignment of the browser.
Border	Specifies the border width, in pixels, of the table.
V Space	Specifies the vertical spacing, in pixels, for the table.
H Space	Specifies the horizontal spacing, in pixels, for the table.
Light Brdr	Specifies the border color to give a highlight effect to the table.
Dark Brdr	Specifies the border color to give a shadow effect to the table.
Bg	Specifies the background image for the table.
Bg	Specifies the background color for the table. (Next to the color list.)
Brdr	Specifies the border color for the table.

Some table properties, such as width and height, can be specified in pixels or as a percentage. By default, they are specified in pixels.

When a table is defined by pixels, it will retain its properties at all times, even when the browser window is resized. The downside to this is that a table cannot adapt to different screen resolutions that viewers might have. On the other hand, when a table is defined by percentages, it will always resize when the browser window is resized, but the actual size of the table might not look as intended.

To modify table properties:

1   Select the cell, row, column, or the table whose properties you want to change.

2   In the Property inspector, from the Brdr list, specify the border color.

3   In the Property inspector, from the Bg list, specify the background color.

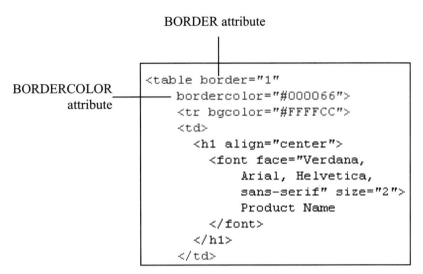

Exhibit 7-10: The HTML code showing TABLE tag attributes

TABLE tag attributes

The TABLE tag has many attributes such as WIDTH, ALIGN, BORDERCOLOR, and BGCOLOR. The WIDTH attribute specifies the width of the table. It can be specified in pixels or as a percentage of the page width. The ALIGN attribute specifies the alignment of the table within a page. The BORDERCOLOR attribute defines the border color and the BGCOLOR attribute defines the background color for the table. Exhibit 7-10 displays some attributes of the TABLE tag.

The TR tags also have their own attributes, such as BGCOLOR and ALIGN. The BGCOLOR attribute defines the background color for the row and the ALIGN attribute defines the alignment of the content of the row.

7–16 Dreamweaver 3.0: Basic

Do it!

B-4: Modifying table properties

Here's how	Here's why
1 Select the table	
2 From the Brdr list, select a dark blue color	CellPad [ ] Align [Default ▾] CellSpace [ ] Border [1] Brdr [■] #000066
	(In the Property inspector, if all properties are not visible, click the expander arrow.) To set the border color for the table.
3 Select the first row	You'll set the background color for this row.
4 From the Bg list, select a light yellow color	Bg [ ] #FFFFCC
	The background color of the first row changes to yellow.
Observe the opening TABLE tag in the HTML code	`<table border="1" bordercolor="#000066">`
	The BORDERCOLOR attribute defines the border color for the table.
Observe the opening TR tag in the HTML code	`<tr bgcolor="#FFFFCC">`
	The BGCOLOR attribute of the TR tag defines the background color for the row.
Close the HTML Source inspector	
Update the document	

Creating tables   **7–17**

Topic C: Resizing cells and tables

Explanation

To give a clean look to a table, you can alter its cells width and the dividers width between cells. The space between the cell content and cell boundary can also be altered. You can also merge cells in a table to extend text across columns or rows.

Width of a column

When you first create a table, the width of the table or column will depend on the content contained in it. If that's not the size you want, you can alter the column width in either pixels or as a percentage of the table width.

You set the column width in one of the following ways:

- In the W property on the Property inspector, enter the value to set the width in pixels.
- In the W property on the Property inspector, enter the value followed by the percent symbol (%) to set the width as a percentage of the table width.
- Select the column and drag the right border of the column.

Do it!

C-1: Changing the width of a column

Here's how	Here's why
1 Select the second column	You'll change the width of this column.
2 In the W box, enter **400**	(In the Property inspector.) To specify the width as 400 pixels.
Press (↵ ENTER)	The width of the column decreases and the text adjusts according to the width of the column.
3 Observe the HTML code	`<td width="400">`
	The WIDTH attribute of the TD tag is used to specify the width of the column.
Close the HTML Source inspector	
4 Update the document	

Cell spacing and cell padding

Explanation

You can also format a table by setting its *cell spacing* and *cell padding*. Cell spacing is the space between the cell content and cell boundary. Cell padding is the width of the dividers between cells. Both of these are specified in pixels.

To change cell spacing and cell padding:

1. Select the table whose properties you want to change.
2. In the CellSpace box of the Property inspector, specify the value for cell spacing.
3. In the CellPad box of the Property inspector, specify the value for cell padding.

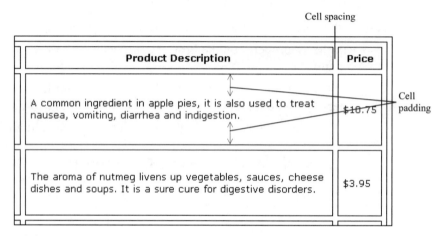

Exhibit 7-11: A portion of the table with cell spacing and cell padding set to 6 pixels

Do it!

C-2: Changing cell spacing and cell padding

Here's how	Here's why
1 Observe the table	The space between the cell content and cell boundary is the cell spacing. The width of the dividers between the cells is the cell padding. You'll change both of these.
Select the table	If necessary.
2 In the CellPad box, enter **6**	To specify the cell padding as 6 pixels.
Press ↵ ENTER	
Observe the table	The cell padding increases.
3 In the CellSpace box, enter **6**	To specify the cell spacing as 6 pixels.
Press ↵ ENTER	
Observe the table	(As shown in Exhibit 7-11.) The cell spacing increases.

4   Deselect the table

    Observe the HTML code

    ```
    <table border="1"
    bordercolor="#000066"
    cellpadding="6"
    cellspacing="6">
    ```

    The CELLSPACING and CELLPADDING attributes of the TABLE tag are used to specify the cell spacing and cell padding.

    Close the HTML Source inspector

    Update the document

Spanning cells

Explanation

You can merge cells horizontally to create a table heading that spans several columns. *Spanning* cells across rows and columns makes it possible to display grouped information in a table. The cells can also be merged to create cells for large graphics.

To merge cells, select the row or the column whose cells you want to merge. Choose Modify, Table, and Merge Cells to merge the cells. You can also use the merge cells button on the Property inspector to merge cells.

Merged cells

Products and their prices		
Product Name	Product Description	Price
Cinnamon	A common ingredient in apple pies, it is also used to treat nausea, vomiting, diarrhea, and indigestion.	$10.75
Nutmeg	The aroma of nutmeg livens up vegetables, sauces, cheese dishes, and soups. It is a sure cure for digestive disorders.	$3.95
Cloves	They can be tasted studded in baked ham, breads, and cakes and in mulled wine. It is used to relieve dental aches and check the symptoms of cholera and asthma.	$8.75

Exhibit 7-12: A table with merged cells in the first row

7–20 Dreamweaver 3.0: Basic

Do it!

C-3: Merging cells in a table

Here's how	Here's why
1 Insert a row at the top of the table	
2 In the second cell of the first row, enter **Products and their prices**	
Set the font to **Verdana, Arial, Helvetica, sans-serif**	Use the Property inspector.
Set the font size to 3 and font style to Bold	Use the Property inspector.
3 Select the first row	You'll merge cells in this row.
Click as shown	(On the Property inspector. This button is used to merge cells.) The text in the first row spans across all three columns.
Center align the text in the first row	As shown in Exhibit 7-12.
4 Observe the HTML code	`<td colspan="3">` The COLSPAN attribute of the TD tag determines the number of columns spanned.
Close the HTML Source inspector	
5 Update and preview the document in the Web browser	
Close the Web browser	

Creating tables　**7–21**

Borderless table

Explanation

By default, Dreamweaver creates tables with one pixel border. At times, you'll need to remove that border so users won't be distracted by it, especially when using a table to create the underlying layout of the Web page. To remove table borders, select the table and on the Property inspector, enter 0 in the Border box.

Products and thier prices		
Product Name	**Product Description**	**Price**
Cinnamon	A common ingredient in apple pies, it is also used to treat nausea, vomiting, diarrhea, and indigestion.	$10.75
Nutmeg	The aroma of nutmeg livens up vegetables, sauces, cheese dishes, and soups. It is a sure cure for digestive disorders.	$3.95
Cloves	They can be tasted studded in baked ham, breads, and cakes and in mulled wine. It is used to relieve dental aches and check the symptoms of cholera and asthma.	$8.75

Exhibit 7-13: A borderless table in the Document window

Do it!

C-4: Removing a table's border

Here's how	Here's why
1　Select the table	You'll remove the table's borders.
2　In the Border box, enter **0**	(In the Property inspector.) To remove borders from the table.
Press ⏎ ENTER	(Refer to Exhibit 7-13.) The table's border is removed.
3　Observe the HTML code	`<table border="0"`
	The BORDER attribute of TABLE specifies the border width of the table.
Close the HTML Source inspector	
4　Update and preview the document in the Web browser	Notice that you can't see the table, but the cell spacing breaks up the background color.
5　Close the Web browser and the document	Do not close Dreamweaver.

Topic D: Using tables to design Web pages

Explanation

One limitation to Web design is that HTML tags will not let you place text and images wherever you want. On the contrary, HTML tags are more concerned with the structure of the page, than how it looks. So, Web designers have had to look for other ways to display their creations in a browser, and the most universal approach has been to use tables without borders.

Nested tables

When designing a page, many Web designers will insert a table inside another table to organize graphics, links, and text the way they want them (as shown in Exhibit 7-14). This table within a table is called a *nested table*. To insert a nested table, place the insertion point in the cell where you want to insert another table and then choose Insert, Table.

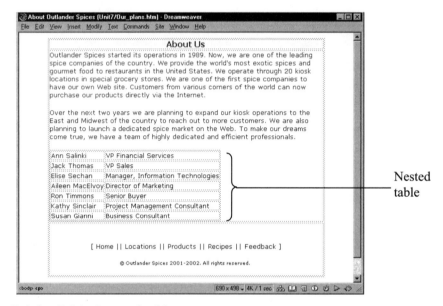

Exhibit 7-14: A nested table

Creating tables **7–23**

Do it!

D-1: Nesting tables

Here's how	Here's why
1 Open Our_plans.htm	In the Unit7 folder.
Place the insertion point as shown	efficient professionals.|
	(At the end of the second paragraph.) You'll insert another table here.
2 Import the table data from Team.txt to this cell	Choose File, Import, Import Table Data and select the text file from the Unit7 folder. The data are separated by semicolons.
3 Set the font of the nested table to Verdana, Arial, Helvetica, sans-serif	
Set the font size of the nested table to 2	
Deselect the nested table	
4 Observe the HTML code	In the code, the TABLE tags are within a pair of TD tags indicating that one table is inserted in the cell of another table.
Close the HTML Source inspector	
5 Select the nested table and remove its borders	Set Border to 0 for the nested table.
Update and preview the document in the Web browser	
Close the Web browser and the document	Do not close Dreamweaver.

Invisible characters and graphics

Explanation

Some browsers display the elements on a page differently, and the results can impact your design. To combat this, many Web designers will use invisible characters or a transparent graphic to maintain control. For example, if you have a table cell that needs to be 50 pixels wide, you have to make sure that all browsers display that cell in the same way. A common practice is to put a transparent GIF file in the cell that has a height of 1 pixel and a width of 50 pixels.

To insert an invisible graphics file in a cell, place the insertion point in the cell whose size you want to fix and insert the invisible image file.

7–24 Dreamweaver 3.0: Basic

Do it!

D-2: Using invisible graphics to control page layout

Here's how	Here's why
1 Open Price_list.htm	(In the Unit7 folder.) The document has a background image.
Observe the text in the first cell of the second row	The text extends over the background image. You'll use an invisible image to correct it.
2 Place the insertion point as shown	
	Click before the text in the cell.
Insert the image transparent.gif	(In the Unit7 folder.) Choose Insert, Image and select the image file.
Observe the image	
	You can only see the boundary of the image.
Set the width of the image to 80 and height to 25	(Use the Property inspector.) The text aligns to the bottom of the invisible image.
3 From the Align list, select **Absolute Middle**	(In the Property inspector.) To vertically align the text to the center of the image.
Observe the text	
	The text's indentation increases and it is now fully visible.
Deselect the image	Click outside the table.
4 Update and close the document	

Creating tables **7–25**

Using tables for page layout

Explanation Most Web site layouts are designed by using tables because they help you align objects, text, and images on a page. Exhibit 7-15 displays a Web page designed by using borderless and nested tables. Tables prevent browsers from altering the size of the Web page to fit the size of the browser window.

Exhibit 7-15: A Web page designed by using tables

Do it!
D-3: Design a Web page by using tables

Here's how	Here's why
1 In a blank document, insert a table with 2 rows and 2 columns	You'll use this table to design the Web page.
2 Merge cells in the first row	
3 Set the title of the document as **Outlander Spices**	In the Page Properties dialog box.
Save the document as **Recipe_page.htm**	In the Unit7 folder.
4 Insert top-panel.gif in the top row	(The image file is in the Unit7 folder.) Place the insertion point in the top row and insert the image.
5 Insert left-panel.gif in the first cell of the second row	The image file is in the Unit7 folder.

6	Place the insertion point in the last cell of the second row	You'll set the width of this cell.
	Set the width of the cell to 400 pixels	In the W property on the Property inspector.
	Set the vertical alignment of the cell to Top	On the Property inspector, from the Vert list, select Top.
7	In this cell, insert a nested table with 2 rows and 2 columns	
8	Insert recipe1.jpg in the first cell of the nested table	The image file is in the Unit7 folder.
9	Insert recipe2.gif in the first cell of the second row of the nested table	The image file is in the Unit7 folder.
10	Enter **Princely Potatoes** in the second cell of the first row of the nested table	
	Enter **Chicken stuffed with spices** in the last cell of the nested table	
11	Insert a row at the top of the nested table	Place the insertion point in the first row of the nested table and insert a row.
	Merge the cells in the row just inserted	
12	Enter **Recipes** in the top row of the nested table	This is the heading for the top row of the nested table.
	Set the format of the text in the top row of the nested table to Heading2 and center align the text	
13	Set a light yellow color as the background color of the top row of the nested table	
14	Set the cell spacing and cell padding to 0 for both tables	

15	Remove the borders from both tables	
16	Link the text Princely Potatoes to **Recipe_1.htm**	In the Unit7 folder.
	Link the text Chicken stuffed with spices to **Recipe_2.htm**	
17	Update and preview the document in the Web browser	You cannot see the underlying table used to design the page as shown in Exhibit 7-15.
18	Close the Web browser and the document	

7–28   Dreamweaver 3.0: Basic

Unit summary: Creating tables

Topic A   In this unit, you learned how to **insert a table** and **add text to it**. You learned how to **insert** and **delete rows and columns** in a table and **import tabular data**. You also learned to **insert images** in a table.

Topic B   Then, you learned how to **select tables**, **rows**, and **columns**, **format table headings**, and **align text in a table**. You also learned how to **modify table properties**.

Topic C   Next, you learned how to **change the width of a column** and the **cell spacing and cell padding** of a table. You also learned how to **merge cells** and **remove a table's border**.

Topic D   Finally, you learned how to **design Web pages** by using **nested tables** and **invisible graphics**.

Independent practice activity

1 Create a blank document.

2 Insert a table with **2** rows and **2** columns.

3 Merge the cells in the first row.

4 Set the title of the document as **Site search page**.

5 Save the document as **Site_search.htm.**

6 Insert top-panel.gif in the top row.

7 Insert left-panel.gif in the first cell of the second row.

8 Set the width of the second column to **500** pixels.

9 Set the vertical alignment of the cell to top.

10 In the second cell of the second row, insert a nested table with eight rows and one column.

11 Enter and format text in the nested table as shown in Exhibit 7-16.

12 Insert and center align the image atwork.gif in the nested table as shown in Exhibit 7-16. (The image is in the Unit7 folder.)

13 Set the cell spacing and cell padding to **0** for both tables.

14 Remove the borders from both tables.

15 Update and preview the document in the Web browser.

16 Compare your work with Exhibit 7-16.

17 Close the Web browser and the document.

Exhibit 7-16: The Site search page after step 15 of the Independent practice activity

7–30 Dreamweaver 3.0: Basic

Unit 8
Creating frames and uploading sites

Unit time: 70 minutes

Complete this unit and you'll know how to:

A Examine a frames page, create a frames page, and set frameset and frame properties.

B Add another frame to a frames page, delete a frame, and create links in a frames page.

C Understand uploading sites and file naming conventions, check and fix links in a site, upload a site, set download time, and open an uploaded site.

Topic A: Working with frames

Explanation

As you surf the Web, you might see the browser window displaying more than one page at the same time and each page enclosed within its own rectangle. These rectangles are called *frames*. The role of frames is to ease navigation and to help users access information.

Frames

Frames help you divide a page into two or more panes. For example, you could create a page that divides the browser window into three panes: a banner at top, a list of products on the left, and a product description on the right. This way the user can see the product list and product descriptions at the same time.

On the Web, you'll see the frames being used in a number of ways:

- A table of contents where creating a link in the left frame displays an associated page in the right frame.
- Search engines where the query form appears in one frame and the results in another.
- Banner advertisement where the banner appears in the top frame on all the pages and the content in the lower frame changes.
- Guestbooks where one frame has the form for visitors' comments; after they click Send, their comments appear in another frame on the same page.

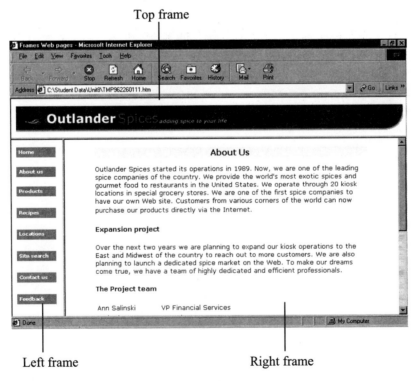

Exhibit 8-1: A Web page with three frames

Creating frames and uploading sites   **8–3**

Do it!

A-1:   Examining frames

Here's how	Here's why
1 Open Frames.htm	(In the Unit8 folder.) You'll examine frames.
Choose **View, Frame Borders**	(If necessary.) The frame borders are now visible.
Preview the document in the Web browser	(As shown in Exhibit 8-1.) The screen is divided into three panes called frames.
2 Scroll down the right frame	The content of this frame scrolls down. The content in the top and left frames remains static.
3 In the left frame, click the **Locations** link	The Locations page appears in the right frame. The content in the top and left frames remains static.
4 View the previous page	Click Back.
Close the Web browser and the document	Do not close Dreamweaver.

The frameset

Explanation

A Web page using frames always has two or more frames on it, and that collection of frames is called a *frameset.* Since you are required to save each frame as an individual HTML file, the frameset is used to define the whole frame layout and is saved as a separate HTML file.

You create a frameset grid by dividing a document into two or more frames. Most Web designers use one frame to hold the main content of the page. The other content, such as the company logo and copyright information, is put in smaller frames at the top, bottom, left, or right of the main frame.

Like tables, frames are another way of setting the layout of a Web page. Typically, Web designers prefer using tables rather than frames because a Web page designed with tables is easier to maintain. For example, to maintain a single page with three frames means maintaining four files: three for individual frames and one for the frameset.

Frames are the best choice when you want one portion of the Web page to remain the same no matter what happens on the rest of the screen. If the page doesn't require an unchanging portion, do not use frames. Use frames only if they make the navigation easy for the visitors. Another point to consider about using frames is that not all browsers support frames.

To create frames:

1   Open a blank document.

2   Place the insertion point where you want the frame to appear.

3   Choose Insert, Frames and then select the position where you want the frame to appear.

4   Activate the frame you want to save.

5   Choose File, Save, specify a frame name and click Save.

6 Save individual frames.
7 Choose File, Save Frameset, specify a name for the frameset, and click Save.
8 Click in any of the frames.
9 Choose File, Open in Frame, select the file you want to open and click Select.
10 Open other frames.
11 Choose File, Save All to save all frames.

Predefined frameset

Dreamweaver provides predefined framesets that you can use to create framesets. You can choose one from the Frames panel of the Objects palette (as shown in Exhibit 8-2).

To display the Object palette, choose Window, Objects. To change the panels on the Object palette, click on the panel menu under the Object palette title bar and choose the appropriate panel.

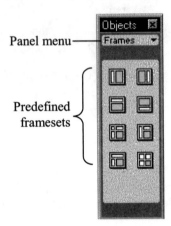

Exhibit 8-2: The Frames panel of the Object palette

Saving a frameset

It is important to save the frameset before you preview the page in the Web browser. By default, Dreamweaver gives a temporary name to the frameset, such as Untitled Frame_1. To save the frameset, choose File, Save Frameset. You can save individual frames by choosing File, Save. To save all files in a frameset, choose File, Save All.

Open an HTML file in a frame

After creating the frameset grid, the frames are empty and you need to put content in them. You can put content in a frame in two ways. One way is to insert text, images, and other objects in a frame just as you would in a blank document. The second way is to open an existing HTML file in a frame. To open an HTML file in a frame, activate the frame by clicking in it and choose File, Open in Frame. Then select the HTML file you want to open and click Select.

The FRAMESET and FRAME tags

The FRAMESET tag along with the FRAME tag creates the frames page. The FRAMESET tags define the outer structure of the frames in a page and have many attributes such as ROWS, COLS, FRAMEBORDER, BORDER, and FRAMESPACING. The ROWS attribute specifies the size and number of the horizontal frames and the COLS attribute specifies the size and number of the vertical frames in a frameset. The size of the rows and columns can be in absolute pixels or percentages. For example, the HTML code in Exhibit 8-3 displays the ROWS attribute as "80*": this means there are two rows; the first row occupies 80 pixels and the rest is occupied by the second row.

The FRAME tags are used inside the FRAMESET tags and define individual frames. The various attributes of this tag are SRC, NAME, NORESIZE, and SCROLLING.

- The SRC attribute of the FRAME tag specifies the document that opens in the frame.
- The NAME attribute specifies a unique name for the frame and is case sensitive.
- The NORESIZE attribute specifies whether the frame can be resized in the browser window.
- The SCROLLING attribute specifies whether the frame has scroll bars.

To view the HTML code for the frames page, you need to select the frameset. You can select a frameset by clicking any of the frame borders. You'll learn more about selecting a frameset later.

```
<frameset rows="80,*" frameborder="NO"
    border="0" framespacing="0">
    <frame name="topFrame" scrolling="NO"
      noresize src="Topframe.htm" >
    <frame name="mainFrame" src="About_us.htm">
</frameset>
```

Exhibit 8-3: The HTML code for the frames page

8–6 Dreamweaver 3.0: Basic

Do it!

A-2: Creating frames

Here's how	Here's why
1 Verify that a blank document is open in the Document window	
Choose **Insert**, **Frames**, **Top**	To split the document into two frames horizontally.
2 Click in the top frame	You'll save this frame.
Choose **File**, **Save**	
Edit the File name box to read **Topframe.htm**	
Click **Save**	To save the frame.
3 Save the bottom frame as **Bottomframe.htm**	Click in the bottom frame and save.
4 Choose **File**, **Save Frameset**	To save the frameset.
Edit the File name box to read **Myframes.htm**	(In the Unit8 folder.) To specify a name for the frameset.
Click **Save**	The frameset name appears on the title bar of the Document window.
5 Click in the top frame and insert Top_panel.gif	
6 Click in the bottom frame	You'll open an existing document in this frame.
Choose **File**, **Open in Frame...**	
Select **About_us.htm**	In the Unit8 folder.
Click **Select**	The document opens in the bottom frame.
7 Choose **File**, **Save All**	To save the frames and the frameset.

Creating frames and uploading sites   **8–7**

8	Click the top border of the top frame	![Commands button with cursor]
		To select the frameset.
	Observe the frameset border	![Commands button with dotted border]
		A dotted border appears.
9	Observe the HTML code	(As shown in Exhibit 8-4.) The FRAMESET tag specifies the layout of the frames in a page. The ROWS attribute specifies the size of the horizontal frames. The FRAMESET tag along with the FRAME tag creates the frames page. The SRC attribute of the FRAME tags specifies the document that opens in the frame.
	Close the HTML Source inspector	
10	Preview the document in the Web browser	The frame borders are not visible. This is the default setting for the frameset.
	Close the Web browser	

Frameset properties

Explanation   Framesets as well as the individual frames have their own properties. You can change frameset properties to provide a distinct look to the Web page. These properties include the width and color of the borders between frames. You can also specify whether you want the frame borders to be visible.

Selecting a frameset

You need to select the frameset to change its properties. You can select the frameset by clicking the frame border in the Document window. The borders of frames within the frameset are outlined with a dotted line. Another way to select the frameset is by using the Frame inspector. To open the Frame inspector, choose Window, Frames. In the Frame inspector, click the frameset border to select the frameset as shown in Exhibit 8-4.

Selected frameset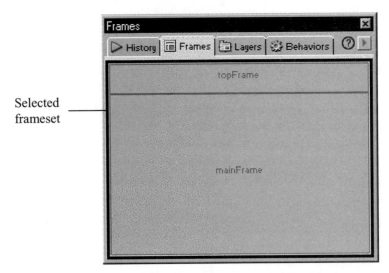

Exhibit 8-4: The Frame inspector showing the selected frameset

To set frameset properties, select the frameset and choose Modify, Page Properties to open the Page Properties dialog box. Set the properties and click OK. You can also set frameset properties in the Property inspector.

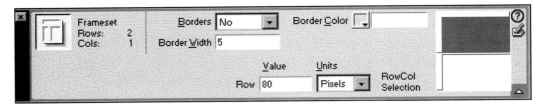

Exhibit 8-5: The Property inspector showing the frameset properties

Creating frames and uploading sites   **8–9**

Do it!

A-3:   Setting frameset properties

Here's how	Here's why
1 Choose **Window**, **Frames**	(If necessary.) To open the Frame inspector.
Click the frameset border	To select the frameset.
2 Set the document title as **My frames page**	In the Page Properties dialog box.
3 Select the frameset	If necessary.
In the Border Width box, enter **5**	(In the Property inspector as shown in Exhibit 8-5.) To specify the border width of the frame.
Press ⟨↵ *ENTER*⟩	The width of the border increases.
4 From the Borders list, select **Default**	(In the Property inspector.) This ensures that the browser determines the appearance of the borders between frames.
5 Observe the HTML code	``` <frameset rows="80,*" border="5" framespacing="5"> ```
	The BORDER attribute of the FRAMESET tag specifies the border width.
Close the HTML Source inspector	
Choose **Window**, **Frames**	To close the Frame inspector.
6 Save the frameset and all the frames	Choose File, Save All.

Frame properties

Explanation

When you use frames, you'll need to organize the page, save the individual frames, and define the frameset. Beyond that, you'll also want to make changes to each frame's individual properties to give it a distinctive look within a Web page. What that means is, you can specify properties for each frame within a frameset. These properties include frame features such as whether it is resizable, has scroll bars, the size of the frame, and the frame margins.

Selecting a frame within a frameset

You can change the properties of frames by selecting them individually. To do so, press the ALT and SHIFT keys and click in the frame you want to select. The frame border will be outlined with a dotted line. You can also use the Frame inspector for selecting a frame. For this, open the Frame inspector and click within the frame or on its borders to select it.

To set properties for a frame, select the frame, and set the properties in the Property inspector.

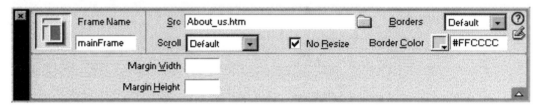

Exhibit 8-6: The Property inspector displaying the frame properties

The following table describes the properties of frames:

Item	Description
FrameName	Specifies a unique name for the frame. It is used while setting it as a target for hyperlinks.
Src	Specifies the source document for the frame.
Scroll	Specifies whether you want scroll bars to appear.
No Resize	Specifies whether dragging the frame borders can alter the frame size.
Border	Specifies the border for the frame. The options are Yes, No, and Default.
Border Color	Specifies a color for the frame border. You can enter the hexadecimal value for the color or use the color list to select a color.
Margin Width	Specifies the left and right margins for the frame. It is specified in pixels.
Margin Height	Specifies the top and bottom margins for the frame. It is specified in pixels.

Do it!

A-4: Setting frame properties

Here's how	Here's why
1 Press `ALT` + `SHIFT` and click in the bottom frame	(To select the bottom frame.) A dotted border appears around the bottom frame.
Observe the Property inspector	It displays the properties of the frame. You'll set the properties for this frame.
2 Check **No Resize**	(In the Property inspector.) To prevent the resizing of the frames in the Web browser.
Set the border color as shown in Exhibit 8-6	
3 In the Margin Height box, enter **0**	To remove the space between the frame's top border and its content.
4 Select the frameset and observe the HTML code	```<frame name="mainFrame" src="About_us.htm" noresize bordercolor="#FFCCCC" marginheight="0">```
	The NAME attribute of the FRAME tag specifies the name of the frame. The NORESIZE attribute specifies that users cannot resize the frame. The BORDERCOLOR and MARGINHEIGHT attributes specify the border color and margin height for the frame.
Close the HTML Source inspector	
5 Update and preview the document in the Web browser	Choose File, Save All.
Close the Web browser	

Topic B: Modifying frames

Explanation

Using frames to design your Web site can be useful. As you become more familiar with them, you'll find out that you modify frames by adding and deleting them from an existing frameset. You can also add links to specific target frames. For example, you can display a table of contents in the left frame that is linked to the corresponding details in the right frame. Any time a user clicks on a link in the left frame, the matching page appears in the right frame.

Nested frames

The more frames you add to a page, the more complex the frame structure becomes. For example, suppose you have a frameset with two horizontal frames (one on top and the other on the bottom) and you want to create another horizontal frame in the middle. Since the page is divided into two frames, if you add another frame to any of the existing frames, it would be a *nested* frame.

To add a nested frame, select the existing frame to which you want to add another frame. Choose Insert, Frames, and then choose the position for the new frame. Save the frame and the frameset.

A nested frames page has a FRAMESET tag enclosed within another FRAMESET tag as shown in Exhibit 8-7.

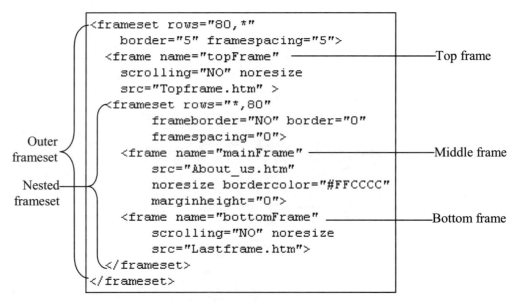

Exhibit 8-7: The HTML code for the nested frame

Creating frames and uploading sites **8-13**

Exhibit 8-8: A nested frames page

Resizing a frame

You can resize a frame in two ways, by using the Property inspector or by dragging the border of the frame. When you use the Property inspector, you can control the frame size by using the Value box and the Units drop-down list as shown in Exhibit 8-9.

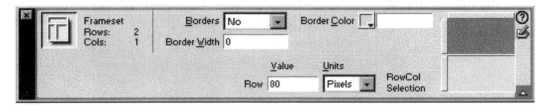

Exhibit 8-9: The Property inspector with frameset properties

You can specify the size of the frame in the Value box. In the case of a horizontal frame, you specify the height in the Value box of the Property inspector as shown in Exhibit 8-9. For a vertical frame, you'll see Column written instead of Row and the value specified will be for the column. By default, the values are in pixels as shown in the Units drop-down list in Exhibit 8-9, and set the selected frame size at an absolute value. The other options are Percent and Relative. If Percent is selected, the selected frame will take the specified percentage of its frameset. The Relative option is the most flexible one and helps in specifying a flexible frame size for different size screens. This option specifies that the selected frame will be allocated space proportional to the other frames.

8–14 Dreamweaver 3.0: Basic

Do it!

B-1: Creating a nested frames page

Here's how	Here's why
1 Click in the bottom frame	(To activate the frame.) You'll add another frame to this frame.
2 Choose **Insert**, **Frames**, **Bottom**	To add another frame at the bottom of the frameset.
Save the bottom frame as **Lastframe.htm**	In the Unit8 folder.
3 Open Bottomframe_text.txt	(In Notepad.) You'll copy its text to the bottom frame.
Copy the entire text	
In the bottom frame, paste it as text	(In the Document window, choose Edit, Paste as Text.) This is the content for the new frame.
4 Set the font of the text to Verdana, Arial, Helvetica, sans-serif	
Align the text to the center	
Set the font size of the first line to 2	
Set the font size of the second line to 1, and the font color to blue	
5 Save all frames	Choose File, Save All.
6 Select the frameset and observe the HTML code	(Refer to Exhibit 8-7.) The ROWS attribute of the inner FRAMESET tag indicates that the bottom frame is divided into two horizontal frames. The value assigned to the ROWS attribute indicates that the new frame occupies 80 pixels and the other frame occupies the remaining height. A FRAMESET tag enclosing another FRAMESET tag creates a nested frames page.
Close the HTML Source inspector	
7 Insert another frame to the left of the middle frame	(As shown in Exhibit 8-8.) Click in the middle frame, choose Insert, Frames, Left.
Save the left frame as **Leftframe.htm**	

8	Open left_list.htm in the left frame	(In the Unit8 folder.) Choose File, Open in Frame and select the file.
9	Select the innermost frameset	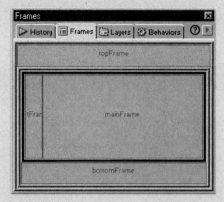
		You'll change the column width of this frameset
	Observe the Property inspector	With the Property inspector expanded, notice the Column Value.
	Drag the border slightly towards the right	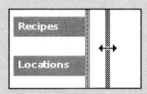
		To increase the width of the left frame.
	Observe the Property inspector	Note that Column Value increases.
	Save all frames	
10	Preview the document in the Web browser	
	Close the Web browser	

Deleting frames

Explanation

Deleting a frame is easy. To delete a frame, select the border of the frame you want to delete and drag the frame border to the edge of the frameset. Remember that the direction you drag the border is important to the frame that is deleted. Once a frame is deleted, you will not be able to undo the action.

8–16 Dreamweaver 3.0: Basic

Do it!

B-2: Deleting a frame

Here's how	Here's why
1 Insert another frame to the right of the middle frame	Click in the middle frame and choose Insert, Frames, Right.
2 Drag the border dividing the middle frame and the right frame to the right until it touches the border of the Document window	

To delete the right frame.

Observe the document   The right frame is deleted.

3 Save all frames

Links in a frames page

Explanation

Creating links in a frame is like creating links in any other Web page. The only thing you need to keep in mind is the target. The target is the place where the linked page will appear. For example, you can have a Web page divided into two vertical frames. In the left frame, you have a list of product names and each name is linked to an individual product page. In this case, when the link is clicked you want the corresponding product details to appear in the right frame. By default, the target page of a hyperlink always appears in the same frame as the hyperlink. To display the target page in a separate frame, you need to specify the name of that frame. So, while creating links in the left frame, you'll specify the right frame's name as the target.

Special target names

You can use special target names to display a linked page in various ways. For instance, to display the target of a hyperlink that links to an external site in another browser window, select _blank from the Target list in the Property inspector. By default, the target is always set to _self, indicating that the target page will appear in the same frame as that of the hyperlink. Some of the target names you can use are _top and _parent. The target name _top opens the link in the entire browser window without the frames. The _parent target opens the link in the *parent frameset*. A parent frameset is the outer frameset when there are nested framesets.

To create links in a frames page:

1 Select the image or text by which you want to create a link.

2 In the Link box of the Property inspector, enter the name of the page to which you want to create a link.

3 From the Target list in the Property inspector, select the frame name in which you want to display the linked page.

Exhibit 8-10: The Property inspector displaying the link and the target

Do it!

B-3: Creating a link in a frames page

Here's how	Here's why
1 From the left frame, select **Locations**	You'll create a link using this image.
2 In the Link box, enter **Location.htm**	You'll create a link to this Web page.
3 From the Target list, select **mainFrame**	(As shown in Exhibit 8-10.) This is the name of the right frame. It will display the contents of the linked document.
4 Observe the HTML code	`<a href="Location.htm" target="mainFrame">`
	The A tag specifies the hyperlink. The HREF attribute specifies the document that is linked. The TARGET attribute specifies the frame name where the linked document will appear.
Close the HTML Source inspector	
5 Update and preview the document in the Web browser	You'll test the link.
Click the **Locations** link	The right frame displays the Locations page.
Go back to the previous page	
Close the Web browser and the document	Do not close Dreamweaver.
Close the Frame inspector	

Topic C: Uploading sites

Explanation

You need to *upload* your Web site on the Internet so that people can access it. Uploading a site refers to copying all of your site's files from your local system to a remote *Web server*. A Web server can be any computer that has Web server software, which is software that supports HTTP, FTP, and other protocols. It makes it possible for a large number of users to access a Web site simultaneously. There are some file naming conventions that you need to keep in mind while uploading sites.

Uploading sites

You need Internet access to host your site on the Web. You also need access to a Web server, which can be through your company, if it has its own Web servers, or through an ISP (Internet Service Provider). The ISP offers space on the Web server. It also offers a range of other services such as site promotion and management. The ISP charge is based on the size and maintenance of the site. You can get information about ISPs by browsing their sites on the Internet. When choosing an ISP, you need to look into its reliability. You also need to inquire about the disk space allocated to your site.

Obtaining a URL

The domain name the ISP offers is very important. For example, a URL like www.outlanderspices.com is easy to remember and also looks professional. You need to pay the domain registration fee in order to register your site. The fees may vary from $20 to $200. The ISP also customarily charges a monthly fee for the maintenance of the site.

File naming conventions

Most Web servers use Unix as the operating system and use file extensions of three or less characters. By default, Dreamweaver adds the file extension .htm to all files saved from the Document window. The normal file extension for a Web page is .html. Almost all Web browsers support .html extensions, but if the server is Unix based, the extension should be .htm. The .htm is the default extension, but your service provider may require you to include .html.

The following are some useful practices for naming files:

- File names should be short and meaningful.
- File names should not start with numbers.
- File names should not contain any special characters such as colons, slashes, periods, and apostrophes.
- File names should not contain any spaces. You can use underscores instead of spaces in file names.

Site Definition dialog box

You used the Site Definition dialog box in earlier units, to create a site, give a name to the site, and specify the location of the local root folder. The Site Definition dialog box is also used to specify Web Server information such as Server Access information. You can choose None, Local/Network, or FTP. None specifies that you do not want to upload your site. Local/Network, specifies that the Web server is on the local network or your local computer is running the Web server. FTP specifies that you want to connect to the Web server by using FTP. If you want to connect using FTP, you need to specify some more information, such as:

- FTP Host name
- Host directory
- Login and password

The Save check box will be automatically selected when you type your password. This ensures that you do not have to enter the password the next time you access the remote FTP site. If you want to enter the password every time you connect to the FTP, clear the Save check box. Check the Use Firewall check box if you want security precautions for the connection between your local network and the Internet.

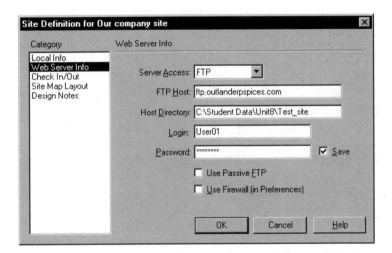

Exhibit 8-11: The Site Definition dialog box

The other options available in the Category list are as follows:

- Check In/Out—This option helps you maintain your files in a multi-user environment.
- Site Map Layout—This option helps in customizing the appearance of the site map. For example, you can change the labels and display of dependent and hidden files in the site map.
- Design Notes—This option helps you in maintaining notes for the Web pages in the site. These notes are stored in a separate file that is attached to the file they refer to.

8–20   Dreamweaver 3.0: Basic

Do it!   **C-1:   Exploring the Site Definition dialog box**

Here's how	Here's why
1 Create a new site called Our company site	
Specify Our_site as the Local root folder	In the Unit8 folder.
2 Close the Site window	
3 Choose **Site**, **Define Sites...**	To open the Define Sites dialog box.
Select **Our company site**	If necessary.
Click **Edit**	To open the Site Definition dialog box.
4 Under Category, select **Web Server Info**	
5 Click the Server Access list	It has options: None, Local/Network, and FTP.
6 From the Server Access list, select **FTP**	Note that more options appear.
7 In the FTP Host box, enter ftp.outlanderspices.com	FTP Host specifies the name of the FTP host where files are uploaded.
8 In the Host Directory box, enter **C:\Student Data\Unit8\Test_site**	Host Directory specifies the path to the remote site.
9 In the Login box, enter **User01**	This is the name used to log in to the FTP server.
10 In the Password box, enter **password**	This is the password used to log in to the FTP server. Asterisks(*) appear in the Password box for security purposes. Both the login and password should be correct to log in to the FTP server.
11 Explore other options in the Category list	
12 Click **Cancel**	To close the Site Definition dialog box.
13 Close the Define Sites dialog box	The Site window opens.

Links in a site

Explanation

When the Web site is ready for upload, it is important to check all the links to ensure that they work. Dreamweaver checks for:

- Broken links
- External links
- Orphaned files

In a Web site, the links are *broken* if you do not update them after moving files from one location to another. The links to Web pages that are external to the Web site are known as *external links*. The Web pages that are not linked to any Web page are known as *orphaned files*.

To check links in a site:

1. Open the site you want to check.
2. Choose Site, Check Links Sitewide to open the Link Checker dialog box.
3. From the Show list, select External Links to view the external links.
4. From the Show list, select Orphaned Files to view the orphaned files in the site.

You fix broken links in the site by changing the URL of the link.

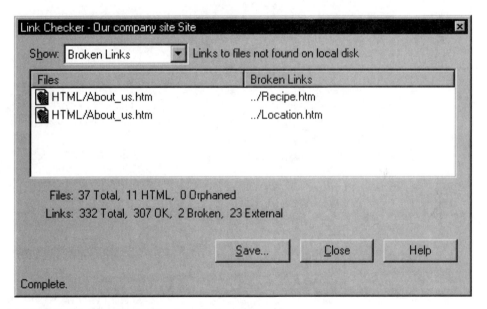

Exhibit 8-12: The Link Checker dialog box

8–22   Dreamweaver 3.0: Basic

Do it!

C-2:   Checking links in a site

Here's how	Here's why
1 Maximize the Site window	If necessary.
2 Choose **Site**, **Check Links Sitewide**	To open the Link Checker dialog box. It shows the process for checking the links in the entire site; then the broken links list appears.
Observe the broken links list	There are two broken links in the site as shown in Exhibit 8-12. Under Files, you'll see a list of files that have broken links. In this case, the links from About_us.htm to Recipe.htm and Location.htm are broken. You'll fix these.
3 Under Files, select **HTML/About_us.htm**	Files Broken Links HTML/About_us.htm ../Recipe.htm HTML/About_us.htm ../Location.htm
Under Broken Links, select **../Recipe.htm**	You'll fix this broken link.
4 Click the folder icon as shown	Broken Links ../Recipe.htm ../Location.htm
	(The Select File dialog box appears.) You'll select the correct path of the file.
Select **Recipe.htm**	It is in the C:\Student Data\Unit8\Our_site\HTML folder.
Click **Select**	
5 Under Broken Link, select **../Location.htm**	Note that the fixed link disappears from the list and the site now has one broken link.
Fix this broken link	Click the folder icon next to the file name and select the correct path of the file. The correct path is C:\Student Data\Unit8\Our_site\HTML.
Click in the blank region in the dialog box	Note that after a while the broken link you've just fixed also disappears. All the broken links are now fixed.
6 From the Show list, select **External Links**	To view the external links list in the site.
7 From the Show list, select **Orphaned Files**	To view the orphaned files list in the site. This site has no orphaned files.
8 Click **Close**	To close the Link Checker dialog box.
9 Close the Site window	

Creating frames and uploading sites   **8–23**

Uploading sites

Explanation

After the site is ready, you need to upload it for people to access it. You can upload the site to a remote server if you have a Web server. You can also upload a site if you have an ISP account.

As discussed earlier, FTP is one of the commonly used methods to upload a site. You can specify the FTP settings in the Preferences dialog box in addition to the Site Definition dialog box. When working in a team, you need to check files in and out. If you are the only developer, you need to put (upload) and get (download) files. When uploading files to the remote system from a folder in the local site, the folder is automatically created on the remote site. The structure of both sites remains the same. You can use the synchronize command to ensure that files in local and remote sites are the latest versions. For this class, you'll upload the site to a remote folder that is present on your system. For uploading the site on the Web server, however, you'll need specific information such as FTP host name, user name and password. You can get all this information from the ISP.

To upload a site to a remote folder:

1 Choose Site, Define Sites to open the Define Sites dialog box.
2 Select the site name.
3 Click Edit to open the Site definition dialog box.
4 From the Category list, select Web Server Info.
5 From the Server Access list, select Local/Network.
6 In the Remote Folder box, specify the path of the remote folder and click OK.
7 Click Done to apply the changes in the site definition.
8 Choose Site, Put to copy files to the remote folder and click OK to transfer the entire site. Click Yes to copy the dependent files also.

Do it!

C-3:   Uploading a site

Here's how	Here's why
1 Choose **Site, Define Sites...**	To open the Define Sites dialog box.
Verify that Our company site is selected	You'll modify this site's definition.
2 Click **Edit**	(To open the Site Definition dialog box.) You'll edit the site's definition.
3 From the Category list, select **Web Server Info**	You'll specify the Web server's information.
4 From the Server Access list, select **Local/Network**	This is the access information of the server where all your site files are stored.

5 In the Remote Folder box, enter **C:\Student Data\Unit8\Test_site** Click **OK**	This is the remote site folder to store all the site files.
6 Click **Done**	To close the Define Sites dialog box.
7 In the Site window, verify that the Our_site folder site is selected	You'll copy all the files from the local folder to the remote folder.
8 Choose **Site**, **Put**	You'll copy the site files from the local folder to the remote site folder. A message box appears asking whether you wish to put the entire site.
Click **OK**	To close the message box and put the entire site. Another message box appears asking you whether to include dependent files.
Click **Yes**	To include the dependent files.
Observe the status bar of the Site window	The status bar shows the file transfer status and indicates that the site files are transferred to the Test site folder.
Verify that both panes of the Site window are visible	
9 Choose **View**, **Refresh Remote**	To view the files in the remote folder.
Observe the left pane of the Site window	It displays all the folders that are put in the remote folder.
Expand all the folders in both panes and compare them	They are the same. This indicates that all the files are transferred to the remote folder.
10 Close the Site window	

Creating frames and uploading sites **8–25**

Download time

Explanation

All Web sites are created on local computer systems and then uploaded to remote Web servers. When you are retrieving a file from the remote system to your local system, you are downloading. While accessing sites on the Web, you might notice that the Web pages appear very slowly. This happens because of a number of factors like the size of the Web page, connection speed of the modem, and Internet traffic at that time. The time the Web page takes to download is known as *download time*. Dreamweaver estimates the document's download time, for different connection speeds, based on its contents, including all linked objects and images. The average connection speed is 28.8 Kilobits per second.

You can set the download time for your document using the Preferences dialog box. To set the download time:

1 Choose Edit, Preferences to open the Preferences dialog box.
2 From the Category list, select Status Bar.
3 From the Connection Speed list, select the desired speed.
4 Click OK.

Do it!

C-4:   Setting the download time

Here's how	Here's why
1 Open Frames.htm	You'll set the download time for this document.
Observe the download time in the status bar	17K / 5 sec
	This is the default download time for the document. It means that 17 KB of the document downloads in 5 seconds.
2 Choose **Edit, Preferences...**	(To open the Preferences dialog box.) You'll change the setting for the download time.
3 From the Category list, select **Status Bar**	To view the settings for the status bar.
4 From the Connection Speed list, select **56**	You'll change the download time for the document by setting this connection speed. Most new modems can achieve this connection speed.
5 Click **OK**	To close the Preferences dialog box.
6 Observe the download time in the status bar	17K / 3 sec
	The new value of the download time appears.
7 Update and close the document	

8–26 Dreamweaver 3.0: Basic

Opening an uploaded site

Explanation

Once you have posted your Web site, you'll need to test it on the Internet. For the purpose of this example, we'll be testing internally. But if you were to post it to an ISP, you would point the browser to the correct address on the Web, such as www.outlanderspices.com to test it.

To open an uploaded site:

1 Start Internet Explorer.
2 Choose File, Open.
3 Select the file you want to open.
4 Click OK.

Do it!

C-5: Opening an uploaded site

Here's how	Here's why
1 Start the Web browser	Choose Start, Programs, Internet Explorer.
2 Choose **File, Open...**	You'll open home page of the uploaded site.
Select **Index.htm**	This file is in the C:\Student Data\Unit8\Test _site\HTML folder.
Click **Open**	
3 Click **OK**	
4 Observe the screen	The home page of the Web site opens in the Web browser.
Browse through the entire site	
5 Close the Web browser	

Creating frames and uploading sites **8-27**

Unit summary: Creating frames and uploading sites

Topic A   In this unit, you learned how to **examine** and **create a frames page**. You also learned how to **set frameset** and **frame properties**.

Topic B   Next, you learned how to **add another frame to a frames page** and **delete a frame**. You also learned how to **create links in a frames page**.

Topic C   Finally, you learned about **uploading sites** and **file naming conventions**. You also learned how to **check** and **fix links in a site**, **upload a site**, **set download time**, and **test an uploaded site**.

Independent practice activity

1 Create a frameset as shown in Exhibit 8-13. (Hint: First create the horizontal frames and then create the vertical frames.)

2 Save the top frame as **firstframe.htm**, left frame as **secondframe.htm**, right frame as **thirdframe.htm**, bottom frame as **fourthframe.htm**, and the frameset as **OurProducts.htm** in the Unit8 folder.

3 Insert Top_panel.gif in the top frame.

4 Open Product_list.htm in the left frame and Cumin.htm in the right frame.

5 Drag the border between the left and the right frame slightly towards the right.

6 Save all the frames.

7 Link the text Coriander from the left frame to **Coriander.htm** and Cumin to **Cumin.htm**. Set the target for both as **mainFrame**.

8 Paste text in the bottom frame from Ipa_bottomframe.txt. Set the text font as Verdana, Arial, Helvetica, sans-serif and center align it. Set the font size of the first line to 2 and of the second line to 1. Set the font color of the second line as blue.

9 Set the Margin Width and the Margin Height of the top frame to 0. (Hint: Select the top frame and set properties in the Property inspector.)

10 Drag the border between the top frame and the right frame so that there is no space between the border and the image in the top frame.

11 Select the frameset and set **Outlander Spices Products** as the title for the page.

12 Save all the frames and preview the document in the Web browser. Compare your work with Exhibit 8-14.

13 Test the links. Close the Web browser and the document. (Do not close Dreamweaver.)

14 Create a site with the name **My_site** by using Unit8ipa as the root folder.

15 Check and fix links in the site.

16 Upload the site to the **C:\Student Data\Unit8\Test_ipa** remote folder.

17 Test the uploaded site.

18 Close the Web browser and the document.

19 Close Dreamweaver.

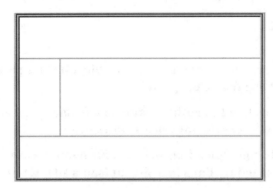

Exhibit 8-13: A frameset layout

Exhibit 8-14: The frames page after step 12 of the Independent practice activity

Dreamweaver 3.0: Basic

Course summary

This summary contains information to help you bring the course to a successful conclusion. Using this information, you will be able to:

A Use the summary text to reinforce what you've learned in class.

B Determine the next courses in this series (if any), as well as any other resources that might help you continue to learn about Dreamweaver 3.0.

S–2 Dreamweaver 3.0: Basic

Topic A: Course summary

Use the following summary text to reinforce what you've learned in class.

Dreamweaver 3.0: Basic

Unit 1

In this unit, you learned **basic Internet** and **HTML concepts**. Then, you learned how to **start Dreamweaver,** explore the **Dreamweaver environment**, and identify the various **components** of the Dreamweaver environment. Next, you learned how to **customize the Dreamweaver environment** and **resize the Document window**. You also learned to **examine the Property inspector** and work with the **History palette**. Finally, you learned to how to **preview a document in the Web browser,** and work with the **HTML Source inspector** and the **Quick Tag Editor**.

Unit 2

In this unit, you learned to **add text, save,** and **edit a document**. Next, you learned how to **set page properties**. Finally, you learned how to **add** and **format a horizontal rule**.

Unit 3

In this unit, you learned how to **format text, insert special characters, ordered** and **unordered lists** in a document. Next, you learned how to insert **paragraph breaks** and **line breaks** in a document and **format paragraph**. You also learned how to **check spellings**. Finally, you learned how to **import text** by using **copy and paste as text** and the **Open dialog box,** and **import and clean up Word HTML documents**.

Unit 4

In this unit, you learned how to **plan a site** and **create a local site**. Next, you learned about the **Site window,** how to **copy site files** to a document and, **move site files** to a folder. You also learned how to **set a home page** and **create a site map**. Finally, you learned how to **create, use,** and **edit a template**.

Unit 5

In this unit, you learned how to **create links to other Web pages, use the drag and drop method to create links,** and about **absolute and relative links**. Next, you learned how to **create named anchors, create link to a named anchor** using the Property inspector, and **the point-to-file method**. Finally, you learned to **create link to external Web sites** and **e-mail addresses**.

Unit 6

In this unit, you learned how to **insert an image, modify the alignment of an image,** and **align text around an image**. Next, you learned how to **add background images**. Finally, you learned how to **create links using an image, create an image map,** and **text label for an image**.

Course summary **S–3**

Unit 7

In this unit, you learned how to **insert a table, add text in it,** and **insert** and **delete rows and columns** in it. Next, you learned how to **import tabular data** and **insert images** in a table. You also learned to **select tables, rows,** and **columns, format table headings** and **align text** in a table. You also learned how to **change the width of a column, change cell spacing** and **cell padding, merge cells,** and **remove borders** of a table. Finally, you learned how to **design Web pages** by using **nested tables** and **invisible graphics.**

Unit 8

In this unit, you learned how to **examine, create a frames page,** and **set frameset and frame properties.** Next, you learned how to **add another frame to a frames page, delete a frame,** and **create links in a frames page.** Finally, you learned about **uploading sites** and **file naming conventions.** You also learned how to **check** and **fix links in a site, upload a site, set download time,** and **test an uploaded site.**

Topic B: Continued learning after class

It is impossible to learn to use any software effectively in a single day. To get the most out of this class, you should begin working with Dreamweaver 3.0 to perform real tasks as soon as possible. Course Technology also offers resources for continued learning.

Next course in this series

This is the first course in this series. The next course in the series is:

- *Dreamweaver 3.0: Advanced*

Other resources

In addition to the other course in this series, you might also find useful additional Course Technology resources as you continue to learn about Dreamweaver 3.0. For more information, visit www.course.com.

Dreamweaver 3.0: Basic

Quick reference

Button	Keystrokes	What it does
B	CTRL + **B**	Applies the bold format to the selection.
I	CTRL + **I**	Applies the italic format to the selection.
▤		Aligns the selection to the left.
▤		Aligns the selection to the center.
▤		Aligns the selection to the right.
▤		Creates unordered list.
▤		Creates ordered list.
	F12	Previews the document in the primary browser.
	CTRL + **F12**	Previews the document in the secondary browser.
	F1	Opens Dreamweaver's help.
	CTRL + SHIFT + **N**	Opens a new document in the Document window.
	CTRL + **O**	Opens a document.
	CTRL + **W**	Closes a document.
	CTRL + **S**	Saves a document.
	CTRL + SHIFT + **S**	Saves all open documents.
	CTRL + **Q**	Closes Dreamweaver.
	CTRL + **Z**	Undo the last action.
	CTRL + **Y**	Redo the last action.

Q–2 Dreamweaver 3.0: Basic

Button	Keystrokes	What it does
	CTRL + **X**	Cuts the selection.
	CTRL + **C**	Copies the selection.
	CTRL + **V**	Pastes the selection.
	CTRL + **A**	Selects all the objects in a document.
	SHIFT + ↵ ENTER	Inserts a line break.
	SHIFT + ↵ ENTER + SPACEBAR	Inserts a non breaking space.
	↵ ENTER	Creates a new paragraph.
	SHIFT + **F7**	Checks spelling.
	CTRL + **J**	Opens Page Properties dialog box.
	CTRL + **T**	Toggles the display of Quick Tag Editor.
	F10	Toggles the display of HTML Source inspector.
	F9	Toggles the display of History palette.
	CTRL + SHIFT + **J**	Toggles the display of Property inspector.
	CTRL + **F10**	Toggles the display of Frames inspector.
	CTRL + TAB	Switches between Document window and HTML Source inspector.

Tag	Description	Attributes
<HTML> </HTML>	Contains the head and body sections of an HTML document	
<HEAD> </HEAD>	Defines head section of an HTML document	
<TITLE> </TITLE>	Creates a title for a Web page	
<BODY> </BODY>	Defines the body of an HTML document	BACKGROUND, BGCOLOR, BGPROPERTIES, LEFTMARGIN, RIGHTMARGIN, TEXT
<H1> </H1>	Creates a first level heading	ALIGN
<H2> </H2>	Creates a second level heading	ALIGN
<H3> </H3>	Creates a third level heading	ALIGN
<H4> </H4>	Creates a fourth level heading	ALIGN
<H5> </H5>	Creates a fifth level heading	ALIGN
<H6> </H6>	Creates a sixth level heading	ALIGN
<P> </P>	Creates a paragraph	ALIGN
  </BR>	Places text on a new line	
<B> </B>	Makes text bold	
<I> </I>	Makes text italics	
<U> </U>	Underlines text	
<FONT> </FONT>	Sets the color, face, and size of text on a Web page	COLOR, FACE, SIZE
<UL> </UL>	Creates an unordered list	
<OL> </OL>	Creates an ordered list	TYPE
<HR> </HR>	Creates a horizontal line across the page	ALIGN, COLOR, NOSHADE, SIZE, WIDTH
<A> </A>	Creates a hyperlink	HREF, NAME
<IMG> </IMG>	Inserts an image	ALIGN, SRC, HEIGHT, WIDTH, HSPACE, VSPACE, BORDER, USEMAP, ALT

Tag	Description	Attributes
<TABLE> </TABLE>	Creates a table	ALIGN, BORDER, WIDTH, BORDERCOLOR, BGCOLOR, CELLSPACING, CELLPADDING
<TR> </TR>	Creates a row in a table	ALIGN, BGCOLOR
<TD> </TD>	Creates a cell in a table	ALIGN, COLSPAN, ROWSPAN, WIDTH
<AREA>	Creates a hot spot on an image map	SHAPE, COORDS, HREF
<MAP> </MAP>	Encloses the definition of an image map	NAME
<FRAMESET> </FRAMESET>	Defines a frameset	COLS, ROWS, BORDERCOLOR, FRAMEBORDER, BORDER, FRAMESPACING
<FRAME>	Defines a frame	SRC, NAME, MARGINWIDTH, MARGINHEIGHT, SCROLLING, NORESIZE, BORDERCOLOR, FRAMEBORDER
<NOFRAMES> </NOFRAMES>	Displays a message for users who view pages with frames in a non-frame supporting browser	

Index

B

Borders, removing, 7-21
Browsers, 1-2

C

Cache files, 4-3
Cells, 7-2
Cells, resizing, 7-17
Cells, spacing, padding, 7-18
Cells, spanning, merging, 7-19
Check Spelling, 3-12

D

Document window, resizing of, 1-8
Documents, check spelling in, 3-12
Documents, creating and editing, 1-14
Documents, formatting, 3-2
Documents, importing text into, 3-14
Dreamweaver, components of, 1-4
Dreamweaver, customizing environment of, 1-6

F

Formatting, font and color in, 3-2
Formatting, line breaks in, 3-6
Formatting, special characters in, 3-5
Formatting, using lists in, 3-8
Frames, deleting, 8-15
Frames, links in, 8-16
Frames, modifying, 8-12
Frames, properties of, 8-10
Frames, resizing, 8-13
Frames, role of, 8-2
Framesets, 8-3
Framesets, properties of, 8-7

H

Home page, 1-2
HTML, basic structure of, 1-16
HTML, Quick Tag for editing of, 1-18
Hyperlinks, 1-2, 4-5, 5-2
Hyperlinks (links), creating, 5-2
Hyperlinks (Links), drag and drop, creating with, 5-4
HyperText Markup Language (HTML), 1-2

I

Image maps, 6-11
Image, alternative to, 6-15
Images, background, 6-8
Images, inserting into table cells, 7-9
Images, on web page, use of, 6-2
Images, properties, modifying, 6-4
Imported HTML text, cleaning up of, 3-16
Importing text, 3-14
Importing text, Open command for, 3-15
Internet, the, defined, 1-2
Internet, World Wide Web distinguished from, 1-2
Invisible graphics, 7-23

L

Links, before uploading, checking, 8-21
Links, e-mail addresses, to, 5-16
Links, frames, in, 8-16
Links, mailto, 5-16
Links, named anchors as, 5-9
Links, paths, absolute and relative, between, 5-7
Links, web sites, to, 5-15

M

Mailto links, 5-16
Mistakes, undoing, 1-11

N

Named anchors, links, as, 5-9

O

Open command, 3-15

P

Page layout, using tables for, 7-25
Paths, absolute and relative, 5-7
Properties, in tables, defined, 7-13

Q

Quick Tag, editing HTML, use of, 1-18

I–2 Dreamweaver 3.0: Basic

R

Resizing frames, 8-13

S

Site maps, 4-10
Site window, 4-5
Site window, copying files in, 4-7
Spelling, documents, check in, 3-12

T

Table cells, inserting images in, 7-9
Table data, importing from other applications, 7-7
Tables, adding text to, 7-4
Tables, cells in, 7-2
Tables, for site layout, using, 7-25
Tables, formatting, 7-11
Tables, headings, 7-12
Tables, nested, 7-22
Tables, resizing, 7-17
Tables, setting properties in, 7-13
Templates, creating, working with, 4-12
Templates, editing, 4-17
Templates, web sites in, 4-2

U

Uploading a site, 8-23
Uploading, checking links ahead of, 8-21
URL (Uniform Resource Locator), defined, 4-2
URL, components of, 5-7

W

Web document, adding colors to a, 2-5
Web document, enhancing a, 2-5
Web page, 1-2
Web page, changing format of text on, 1-9
Web page, editing a, 2-4
Web page, hyperlinks in, 1-2
Web page, images in, 6-2
Web site, navigation in a, 4-2
Web site, planning of, 4-2
Web site, uploading a, 8-18, 8-23
Web sites, Dreamweaver, creating with, 2-2
Web sites, linking to, 5-15
Web sites, web pages in, 1-2
World Wide Web (WWW), browsers for, 1-2
WWW, services on, 1-2